How to Improve Student Learning

A GUIDE FOR Parents, Teachers, Students, *or* Anyone Interested in Education & Learning

George P. Waldheim, Ed.D.

Revised Version

How to Improve Student Learning
(Revised Version)

Copyright 2022, Author: Dr. George P. Waldheim,
Casa Grande, Arizona

ISBN: 978-1-7348450-3-7 Paperback
ISBN: 978-1-7348450-4-4 Hardcover

First published and printed in the United States in 2021, (Revised 2022). All rights reserved. No part of this publication may be reproduced or distributed, in any form or by any means, or stored in a data base or retrieval system without the prior written permission of the author.   Email: towally38@gmail.com

Book and cover design: Deborah Stocco, MyBookDesigner.com

Disclaimer: This text is designed to provide information for all concerned people who are committed to improving learning in schools and colleges. It is published under the expressed understanding that any decisions or actions taken as a result of reading this publication must be based on your personal judgment and will be your sole responsibility. The author will not be held responsible for the consequences of any actions and/or decisions taken by others as a result of any information given or recommendations made.

Notes: The Examples described in this text are all real as experienced by the author. The names, dates, and locations have been changed and/or omitted to protect privacy and identity. In addition, the terms "Teacher" and "Educator" are used throughout this text to simplify the various position titles of those involved in teaching others.

Dedication

Students are not learning to public expectations in U.S. public schools and colleges. Improvement in learning is necessary to resolve the following realities: The U.S. has a mediocre world ranking in public education, extreme national and large city drop-out rates, exploding public school student exodus movement, low test scores, and unpopular national learning initiatives.

These realities confirm there are consequential problems with public school learning thus this Guide is dedicated to explaining *What the problems are, Why the problems exist, and How to improve student learning.*

This Guide is also dedicated to helping Parents, School Board Members, Administrators, Teachers, Students or anyone interested in the education of others promote the improvements needed.

It is logical that learning is the result of teaching, thus the challenge of the educator will be to improve those practices that will improve student learning, especially ensuring the learning of those not learning.

By applying the world-proven practices described in this Guide, those involved in the education of others will create a learning environment recognized as the preferred school, and the school's classes, courses, or subjects to take; rather than avoid.

Thus, the Guide: *How to Improve Student Learning*.

Table of Contents

Acknowledgements................................. ix
Author Biography................................. xi
Preface xiii

    Reality #1: Mediocre International Ranking and Excessive National Drop-Outs xiii
    Reality #2: Large City Drop-Outs and Dissatisfied Stay-Outs.. xiv
    Reality #3: School Exodus Movement and Failing Initiatives xv
    Reality #4: Effectiveness of Public versus Proprietary Learning xvi
    The Intention of: *How to Improve Student Learning* xviii

Introduction 1

    The Consumer's Perception of Education 1
    Public Education and Business........................ 2
    The Competitive Need for Improvement 4

Chapter 1: Realities of Traditional Learning 7

    The Results of Reality 7
    Retaining Perception Memories 9
    The Concept for Improving Learning 11
    The Necessity for Improving Learning 15
    Teaching Versus Training 17
    The Result of Improvement 18
    Traditional Expectations........................... 19
    Traditional Error In Learning Reinforcement 21
    Improvements...................................... 23

Chapter 2: Methods for Learning 25

    How We Learn 25
    Learning Reception and Retention.................... 27
    Traditional Learning Dilemma....................... 29

Learning with the Learning Dilemma 32
How to Ensure Learning............................36
Teacher's Influence on Learners.....................41
Improvements....................................43

Chapter 3: Responsibility and Accountability for Learning... 45

Responsibility for Learning 45
Learning and Accountability 46
Learning with Measurable Objectives 49
Learning with Standardized Testing..................51
Developing the Interest to Learn 53
Learner Performance and Learning Improvement 56
Complimenting the Use of Textbooks 57
Responsibility and Accountability 58
Improvements....................................59

Chapter 4: Preparation for Student Learning 63

The Learning Plan 63
Topic Objective 64
Methodologies for Learning........................66
Analysis of Learning 70
Improved Methodologies 73
Focus on Learning 77
Improvements....................................78

Chapter 5: Evaluation of Students.....................81

Evaluation.......................................81
Methods of Evaluation 83
Student Grading 85
Curve Grading 87
Evaluation for Improvement 89
Improvements....................................91

Chapter 6: Elimination of Gender Bias.................93

Gender Bias 93
Gender Bias at Home..............................94
Gender Bias at School 95
Advisement Bias..................................97

Advisement and Gender Bias........................101
Teacher's Gender Bias............................102
Improvements....................................104

Chapter 7: Ethics and Teacher's Responsibilities.......107

Ethics..107
Teacher Responsibilities.........................108
Improvements....................................111

Chapter 8: Evaluating Teachers.....................113

The Traditional Process..........................113
Public Demand for Accountability..................116
Evaluation Accountability........................117
Evaluate For Student Learning.....................120
Public Perception...............................122
Improvements....................................123

Chapter 9: Teacher Contracts.......................127

Contract Types and Content.......................127
Probationary Contract............................**127**
Continuing Contract (Tenure).....................129
Accountability For Student Learning...............134
Relating Contracts to Student Learning............135
Improving Tenure................................137
Improvements....................................140

Chapter 10: Management of Teachers.................143

Administration and Management....................143
Evaluation......................................144
Final Student Evaluations........................146
Current Faculty Evaluation.......................148
Perception of Improvement........................151
Acceptable Level of Learning.....................153
Improvements....................................155

Chapter 11: Teacher Education.....................157

Education Programs and Structure.................157
Traditional Teacher Education Programs...........158

Effective Teacher Education Programs................161
Interpreting Test Results...........................163
Relationship of Necessity and Learning...............165
Improvements.......................................166

Chapter 12: Procedures to Improve Student Learning...169

Chapter 1: Realities of Traditional Learning 169
Chapter 2: Methods for Learning.....................170
Chapter 3: Responsibility and Accountability for Learning 170
Chapter 4: Preparation for Student Learning 171
Chapter 5: Evaluation of Student Learning 172
Chapter 6: Elimination of Gender Bias 172
Chapter 7: Ethics and Teacher's Responsibilities.........173
Chapter 8: Evaluation of Teachers 173
Chapter 9: Teacher Contracts........................174
Chapter 10: Management of Teachers 175
Chapter 11: Teacher Education.......................176
Chapter 12: Procedures to Improve Student Learning....177
Chapter 13: Improving Student Learning...............177

Chapter 13: Improving Public Education...............179

Advantage of Improvement 179
Necessity for Improvement 180
The Solution to Improve Student Learning 182

Acknowledgements

The initial motivation to write this Guide was generated by the author's experiences working with and administratively reviewing a large number of teachers across various disciplines. The commonalities of effective teachers, coupled with their mutual dedication to improve student learning, served as incentive for this text.

Additional motivation was generated by the current reality of students exiting public elementary and highschools to alternative education offerings such as charter schools, private schools, and home schooling. The message is clear: The traditional public school system is not meeting the learning expectations of many students and parents.

This response, *How to Improve Student Learning*, acknowledges all those who the author has encountered who experienced the trials of being a Parent, School Board Member, Administrator, Teacher, Student, or any one interested/involved in public education—the resultant learning,and their desire for a better experience. It is a Guide for improvement.

Finally, it is without hesitation that the author acknowledges the significant support of his wife Carol, and daughters Kate and Marjorie, and their unending commitment to helping others learn.

Thanks to all.

Author Biography

The author, Dr. George P. Waldheim, spent the first half of his career in private business and the second half in public education. Formal education includes an Associate Degree from Erie County Technical Institute (currently Erie Community College) Williamsville NY, Bachelor and Master of Science Degrees in Education from Buffalo State College, State University of New York (SUNY) Buffalo NY, Doctorate in Education from the University at Buffalo (SUNY) Buffalo NY.

The author began teaching in the Military; afterward teaching and administering a wide variety of classes from church school to two-year College, four-year College, and then the University. Positions included: Sergeant—US Marine Corps Training Command. Co-owner of a Manufacturing Company in Buffalo NY. Associate Professor at the University of Nebraska-Omaha/Lincoln NE. Professor and Department Chair at California State University-Chico CA. Dean of Business and Technology at College of the Redwoods-Eureka CA and Dean of the College of Technology at Ferris State University-Big

Rapids MI. Personally, the author and his wife parented two children from kindergarten to college to the world of work.

The author's service includes: Rotarian Eureka CA. President Small Business Development Center (SBDC) Humboldt and Del Norte Counties CA. Vice President CA Community Colleges Association of Occupational Education (CCCAOE) North/Far North Region. Chair CA North Coast Articulation Council. Regional Accreditation Reviewer for Northwest Association of Schools and Colleges-Seattle WA.

Awards include: Award of Excellence for outstanding achievement in education, research, and service to students *"Teacher of the Year"* by the College of Engineering & Technology, Halliburton Education Foundation, University of Nebraska-Omaha/Lincoln. "Professor Emeritus" California State University Chico.

Prior Professional Memberships: Society of Manufacturing Engineers (SME). Chair, American Society for Engineering Education (ASEE) Midwest Section Engineering Technology Division. National Association of Industrial Technology (NAIT).

Preface

Question: Why a Guide entitled "How to Improve Student Learning?"

Answer: Improvement is necessary to resolve the following Realities—they are descriptive of "What the problems are."

Reality #1
Mediocre International Ranking and Excessive National Drop-Outs

THE REALITIES BEGIN WITH THE international ranking of the United States (U.S.) in education; commonly described as "mediocre" yet the U.S. is the world's leader in manufacturing, military, food production, space exploration, etc. In addition, the U.S. high-school dropout rate is extremely high and reported SAT test scores (college admissions) are inexplicably low. Depending upon where the information comes from, the government or the private sector, the reported number of high-school drop-outs in the U.S. appears to range between 2.5 to 3 million students per year from a total enrollment of 15.3 million. This number equates to approximately 7,500 students dropping out of high-school each day. The structural drop-outs, those who unavoidably relocate or have financial issues, generally amount to only 3 to 4 percent of the 18 percent total. The balance of 15 percent have made their drop-out decision based on their experience.

At the college level, the number of reported drop-outs is slightly less than 2 million students per year—or approximately 5300 students per day. The combined total equates to 12,800 students dropping out of both high-school and college in the U.S. each day of the calendar year. The seriousness and magnitude of the numbers is difficult to perceive until one visualizes that in just six days (less than a week) the number of drop-outs from U.S. schools and colleges would fill the Astrodome Stadium in Houston Texas to over capacity; in just six days—and that continues all year long.

Nationally a huge number of enrolled students are decidedly walking out on the U.S. system of public education.

REALITY #2
LARGE CITY DROP-OUTS AND DISSATISFIED STAY-OUTS

It is also a reported reality that in the 50 largest U.S. cities only 59 percent of students graduate from high-school leaving 41 percent who drop-out or never finish. Unfortunately drop-outs are not eligible for the vast majority of jobs in the U.S. and, as a matter of record, commit the most crimes in the U.S. It appears that school drop-outs are fueling both crime and unemployment. In addition to the drop-out dilemma there are the unreported stay-outs; those who have gone through the system, survived bad learning experiences, and have vowed to never return unless forced; in many cases a requirement of employment prevails. Their number is indeterminable but they exhibit a highly vocalized force in public discussion concerning their questionable classroom memories. Put together, large city drop-outs and stay-outs, that's a very large number of potential learners who have called it quits on the U.S. system of public education.

Reality #3
School Exodus Movement and Failing Initiatives

Another reality is demonstrated by an increasingly motivated student exodus movement from the traditional elementary and secondary schools (high-schools) to charter schools, various private schools, and home schooling. This movement is gaining serious national momentum (some cities characterize it as "exploding") and strongly verifies that student learning is not improving. This exodus movement demand has become so strong that it is now being promoted by some States who are subsidizing the student's transfer with the originating school's district funds—a designated amount per student that the student takes with them towards the cost of the alternative education. Students as well as parents are disenchanted and both are currently engaged in searching for alternative student learning opportunities.

Additionally, there is continuous public and political agreement that the U.S. system of public education has discernible problems and band-aid improvements such as new initiatives and more dollars are not proving to improve student learning. Critics of education are profound in emphasizing that prior national incentive type initiatives have not significantly improved the education dilemma. Unfortunately, that perception is somewhat accurate in that the U.S. continues to maintain a mediocre international education ranking, low SAT scores, high drop-out rates, and an indeterminable number of dissatisfied stay-outs.

REALITY #4
EFFECTIVENESS OF PUBLIC VERSUS PROPRIETARY LEARNING

Reality also points to the learning differences experienced in public education (schools and colleges) versus those experiences outside of schools and colleges.

In public education the emphasis is on teaching; expecting students to learn the way the teacher teaches. This emphasizes the single learning mode of Hearing (listening and reading) with teacher accountability justified by a diverse spread of student grades; depicting high grade reward and low-grade penalty. This traditional focus of learning is questionably ineffective; the outcome verified by the aforementioned realities.

Outside of public education (proprietary/business, corporate classes, short courses, etc.) the emphasis is on learning; expecting teachers to teach the way students learn. This emphasizes the multi-modes of learning with instructional accountability justified by continuously analyzing student learning and then making teaching methodology improvements for subsequent teaching. This is called "continuous improvement;" the goal being to produce higher and less diversity in grades and easier learning for all. This concept of learning is much more efficient, thus more effective, and is proven necessary in a competitive and accountable market.

To improve student learning in schools and colleges and position the U.S. as a leader in world education there needs to be significant improvement in the way students learn.

The Intention of: How to Improve Student Learning

The realities of a low world ranking in education, extreme national and city drop-out rates, highly vocalized stay-outs, a public-school exodus movement, failing initiatives, and the perceptive difference in the effectiveness of public versus proprietary learning—all verify serious issues with student learning in the U.S. Resultantly this affects our ability to successfully prepare citizenry through public education (4.5 million drop-outs per year) and indicates it's necessary to apply solutions.

The intention of this Guide is to improve student learning. It is written to help Parents, School Board Members, Administrators, Teachers, Students, or anyone interested in the education of others promote the improvements needed.

> Readers are advised to apply those parts of this Guide that will promote improvement in student learning and educate more effectively.

Because this is a working Guide, room for notes is provided (one or two pages at the end of each Chapter) for the reader to note their applications of the Chapter information.

The format for this Guide begins with the Preface which reviews the compelling realities created by the problems in

U.S. public schools. *"What the problems are."*

The Introduction and Chapter 1 relate to *"Why the problems exist."*

Chapters 2-7 present proven solutions—*"How to improve student learning."* These solutions are the guide to improving learning and are established on millennium proven methodologies of learning and the world proven process of continuous improvement. Again, the text is written as a Guide to improve student learning.

The following Chapters 8-11 focus on supervisory and administrative responsibilities and improving teacher education programs. This includes the implementation of procedures necessary to manage, maintain, and teach improvement in student learning.

The final Chapters 12-13 collectively outline what should change to significantly improve student learning. That is what this Guide is all about.

In addition, the terms "Teacher" and "Educator" are used throughout this Guide to simplify the identity of anyone teaching or educating others in lieu of their actual academic employment title such as Substitute, Assistant, Aide, Part-Time, Adjunct, Instructor, Assistant Professor, Associate Professor, Full Professor, Mentor, or Administrator.

Note that the practices described in this Guide will be accomplished over time; beginning in the classroom with various teaching methods, analyzing the student learning derived from those methods, and planning methodology improvements for subsequent teaching—all on a continuous basis. This is how our society has made significant advancements/improvements in short periods of time—it is a world proven methodology. The reality is that without a process of continuous improvement resultant student learning remains similar, year after year. Thus, numerous years of teaching experience realistically relate to one year of real experience and the remaining years of similar repetition. The results of this have been recognized by the public, government, students, and parents. These groups have been emphatically searching, and are now creating, alternative solutions.

Preface Numerical References: Statistic Brain Research Institute, College Scorecard of the U.S. Department of Education—National Center for Education Statistics—Hechinger Report, U.S News.

Notes:

Notes:

Introduction

This introduction is a preliminary look at "Why these problems exist" including the reactions of an ever-changing society of consumers and the effect it is having on teaching and student learning in the U.S.

The Consumer's Perception of Education

Outside of Public Education: Consumers pay a seller for the product they sell. If their product does not work, consumers get it repaired/replaced, or get their money back.

Within Public Education: Consumers (taxpayers) pay a teacher for students to learn what they teach. If learning is poor, students are penalized (low grades) and the consumer's money is gone.

Consumers Perception: To the public (increasing number of students, parents, lawmakers, funding agencies, and critics, etc.) this is contrary to the existing consumer's market but is the reality of the current system.

In response there is increasing litigation against the

public system of education indicating that consumers are seeking accountability as well as being driven to find alternative learning opportunities.

PUBLIC EDUCATION AND BUSINESS

Business (as dictionary defined) is a "specific pursuit," an "occupation in which one is engaged," "commercial, industrial, or professional." A teacher is a professional occupation certainly engaged in the specific pursuit of student learning. In reality the fundamental difference between education and business is whether administered public (non-profit) or private (for-profit); consumer money supports both for specific pursuits. However:

Outside of Public Education, when problems occur with whatever is produced, they have to be solved. If the problems are not solved whatever is produced becomes unmarketable and the business entity loses money. If the business loses too much money it goes out of business, so the emphasis has to be on solving problems in order to keep current, marketable, and to stay in business.

Within Public Education it appears to the consumer that when problems occur, with the most important product *student learning,* the reality is to place the responsibility on the consumer (the student); they don't listen, they don't do the work, etc. The public perception is that the system avoids any process changes necessary to fix the learning problems by relating "We have no control over what the student does." Again, the practices are repeated all over with a new class or semester. Minimal process is given to resolving the problem of poor student learning except to issue penalty poor grades. The reality is that the public education entity does not go out of business when learning depreciates thus the problems persist, and time evolves, and the end result is a matter of public record—student learning does not significantly improve.

Therefore, the sole purpose of this text is to improve student learning. Note that the difference between students dropping out of school or being a success in school is, more often than not, based on their experience. With good experiences they tend to stay, with too many bad experiences they go, good coupled with bad the students adapt to reality to complete their program. Rest assured improvement in education is not a one-time solution, or specifically, more money related. It is a learning related issue and will require improvement in practices that are significantly traditional. Educators will redirect a system that admittedly can never be perfect, but can and will be one of the best in the world.

THE COMPETITIVE NEED FOR IMPROVEMENT

How did transportation go from the early bare-bones cars to the luxurious models of today? How did medicine go from treating the cause to preventing the cause? How did communications go from the radio to multi-mode information technology? How did. . .? Answer: by analyzing what was produced and continuously improving it for ever changing competitive needs: physical, technological, and societal.

How did education go from the early 1900's educator standing in front of a class "preach teaching" to today's educator standing in front of a class preach teaching? This was accomplished because in the public system of education there is not a process that evaluates student learning specifically for improving the teaching methodologies—to improve student learning. The lack of a need to continuously improve promotes, perpetuates, and magnifies ingrained practices resulting in unresolved problems and ineffective student learning.

Individuals in the profession of education are becoming increasingly aware that students and the general public are considering themselves to be front line consumers and thus perceive they have a purchaser's right of inquiry and logical obligation to hold their school board, administrators, and faculty accountable for the productivity of their product—student learning.

Introduction

Example: When the public purchases food all the product ingredients (nutrition facts) and performance level of the product (calories) are lawfully revealed for their decision making. When the public purchases education the specific course outcomes (information expectations) and performance level of instruction (instructional effectiveness) are generally unavailable.

It is becoming an ever-increasing reality that the funding parties (both government and public) expect the course outcomes and the performance level of instruction for effective planning and decision making. Therefore, to be sure the public and the U.S. system of education have the most effective course ingredients and performance levels will require combining both the millennium proven practices of multi-mode learning and the world proven process of continuous improvement.

> The real-life examples subsequently described in this text reinforce the need to provide an improvement guide for public education consumers (parents, students, teachers, and others).

The questions most persistently asked by the public about improving education are: ***What do we need? Why don't we have it? How can we get it? Read On.***

Notes:

Chapter 1: Realities of Traditional Learning

The traditional way students learn in U.S. public schools has evolved and reinforced itself over years of repetition. Concurrently the growth of learning problems derived from this has not been successfully responded to. The resultant Realities necessitate improvement.

To the Reader: Apply the improvements related in "The Realities of Traditional Learning" that will improve student learning.

The Results of Reality

Example: A retired educator had his hair cut at a place similar to "Super Cuts." Being new to the area he asked the young stylist if she was familiar with the area to which she replied that she "was born and raised here." The educator then asked her about the local schools to which she replied, in a furious manner, they are terrible. Her story described the home high school as so "chaotic" that her mother enrolled her in the alternative charter school in their area. Her description of the charter school was worse in that the study hall had about 50 students in it and if you had a question you had to write it on the white board from which the teacher would attempt answers in numerical order. She said there were always about 45 questions on the board but the teacher could only answer about 15 of them (hers were in the 30's numerical sequence) and then the period would be over. After numerous study hall attempts to get answers to her questions she walked out of the school in frustration, went home, and asked her mother to home school her. Subsequently she went job hunting and became a stylist; a positive opportunity at the end of a sad educational experience. Obviously, there is much more to this than described here but her concluding perception of her high school education experience (student learning) was dramatically unacceptable. She had been a stylist for approximately 2 years and was successful at her location; meaning she was able to learn and be successfully productive in her profession but on the other hand could not be successful in a public high school, professional led education, that was a responsibility of the State.

The U.S. City of her location has a population of approximately 530,000 people. The published data indicates there are a total of 143 public and private schools of which 99 are charter schools. There are more charter schools than district public schools. That raises the question of why? What is it that motivates students/parents to move from their public schools to alternative schooling? It logically must relate to learning and an unfavorable effect.

Chapter 1: Realities of Traditional Learning

Retaining Perception Memories

If a student doesn't learn do not be so quick to blame the student. Most students who initially enter a class have the mental disposition to want to complete and/or do well in the class. Those who enter a class with a preconceived notion of difficulty or failure have already contracted that notion from previous poor learning experiences. Thus, it appears it would be the system's responsibility to repair, however the traditional practice appears to justify the student's future difficulty or failure by relating to their past performance so students are advised to go somewhere else or are given their well-deserved "F." This "kick the can down the road" solution to student learning problems tends to get worse and results in greater student alienation of the system; more drop-outs and more stay-outs. An overwhelming number of community college students, when interviewed, expressed similar experiences. First, they did poorly in high school because it was just not interesting, didn't make sense, and they did not learn well. Additionally, they felt ignored and attention was given to the better learners. Thus, they developed a poor perception of themselves; some to the point they relate being told "It's too bad you can't learn." Now, later in life they realize, mostly because of success in their job (they learned how to learn by seeing and doing), they come back to school in spite of the prior damage inflicted. Unfortunately, recognizable damage occurs and this is the direct result of existing learning practices. Had the system been accountable for analyzing what the students should have learned, the problem being exposed by analyzing low test scores, those problems could have been preventively planned from repeating themselves through a process of continuous learning improvement. However, situations like this persist, magnify, and tend to go on year after year. When returning students are interviewed, many times the same names of those inflicting the damage re-occur.

Many older adults still have nightmares about a class, or classes, they took 20, 30, to even 40 or 50 years ago. When asked: "Was it interesting, made sense, gave you the feeling of accomplishing learning that will help you?" they laughed and said, "Just the opposite." For too many students the educational system did serious perception damage. The community college enrollments are filled with students whose prior education experience (elementary and high-school) was much less than satisfactory.

Example: A faculty member reported to the Department Head that there was a student problem she uncovered in class that required administrative attention. The class was a first-year college course in writing and the faculty member said she had two students (related brothers) that could not write a sentence. The Department Head questioned whether the problem was in sentence structure, spelling, or what. The faculty member respectively said you do not understand—the two students cannot write at all. The teacher said she gave an in-class writing assignment to all her students and the two brothers could not write—could not write at all.

Upon investigation the two brothers had taken ESL classes (English as a Second Language) in the local high school from where they graduated and were admitted to the first year of college based on their high school graduation. Further investigation revealed that the brothers had all of their high school English assignments completed by others, as well as their final English examinations. The Principal of their high school indicated that this was possible as their final examination identity check was not that specific—as well as their cumulative course assignments.

The brothers were removed from the enrolled class and re-enrolled in an ESL class that was taught by an adjunct faculty member. The high school preparation of these two students was dramatically lacking which tends to question the preparation of the remaining students. Evaluation of learning and continuous improvement are essential to improving student learning.

THE CONCEPT FOR IMPROVING LEARNING

It is necessary to improve the current teaching methodologies if we want to become a world leader in education. Specifically, to improve the level of student learning means improving the way students learn. In the classroom there is only a teacher and the students. Theoretically, if we take away the teacher then no learning occurs. Therefore, the teacher, when teaching, causes learning to take place. **The level of this learning can and should be documented; it is the baseline for instructional improvement.**

Learning happens in an environment of varying applications of student abilities, interests, dispositions, feelings, etc., much of which is in reaction to teaching. If teaching is a process that is continuously improved then learning will improve, as well as the student perception and value of learning. Only then will the U.S. be able to reduce the drop-out and stay-out rates, and be able to improve an educational system currently focused on other priorities.

The reality is that traditional teaching is too significantly based on what can be characterized as lecture-telling—utilizing the single learning mode of Hearing (listening and reading). To the counter-argument "Not necessarily so because we use computers," the reply has to be "No." Computers, currently and for the most part, have not changed the lecture methodology. Students read the computer screen, on which they are seeing words/numbers etc., and then go about repeating it to themselves as if they heard it from the lecturer's mouth; thus, the students are lecturing to themselves.

How effective is the lecture-telling method? Look at life situations. As a parent I told them not to do it but they just wouldn't listen. As a friend I warned them but they

Chapter 1: Realities of Traditional Learning

just didn't listen. As a whatever—. The way information is sent, received, and effectively learned is dramatically different today than it was 20, 10, or even a few years ago? If so, why haven't we dramatically changed the way we teach? In the spirit of answering this question it is necessary to first ask ourselves: How do I remember things best? By Hearing it? Seeing it? or Doing it? The truthful answer exposes the dilemma; U.S. schools and colleges are not adapting to the way students learn best.

Teaching, mostly by lecture-telling (learning mode of Hearing and reading) is conventional yet inefficient in that it tends to eliminate the more effective learning modes of Seeing and Doing. This is deceptively justified by the system's interpretive grading practice (high scores-high effort, low scores-low effort) and thus unwittingly protects this inefficient and less effective teaching methodology. Additionally, there is a system wide lack of requiring analysis of learning for planning continuous improvement, even when justified by documented poor student learning. Do you want to know who the better teachers are? Just ask the students. They know because they are the products being produced. They have the real experience of what is being learned and at what level.

Example: One institution's school bookstore had its glass windows completely covered with each faculty member's previous class student evaluation summary page. The students would read the scores and make decisions on what classes to take, based on the scores. The next semester all evaluation summaries were removed and thus the problems hidden.

In reality, it is perceived by the public that the public is paying for learning and logically has an invested right to see what they receive for their money. The current teaching accountability practice appears to be quite dissimilar to the way it was hundreds of years ago because then the teachers/lecturers would walk down an aisle and the students would put teaching payment money in the frock-tail rear pouch of their lecture robe. The teacher/lecturer would be paid according to their student's perception of their learning. Years ago educators were more directly accountable for student learning because payment was directly related to their performance; that is, how the students perceived their learning. Today, in reverse, student learning is held accountable by critical ranges of grades. Therefore, accountability for student learning was shifted to the students and evolved away from the educator. This accountability, meaningfully reversed and now a tradition, has resultant effects on student learning. *The most critical effect is that this has not promoted instructional motivation to improve student learning.*

Chapter 1: Realities of Traditional Learning

The Necessity for Improving Learning

Currently, the public teaching and learning system is not structured to respond with continuous instructional improvement to measured student learning. As revealed in the following chapters, the system unwittingly hides the problems and promotes the extension of them. Educators, to improve learning, will first evaluate at what level the students have learned the class material, and second, make continuous changes to the methods of instruction in order to improve learning. The important point will be the level of student learning considered acceptable; not grades on any curve, but a straightforward score and documentation of what the students have learned in the class versus what the students were supposed to have learned in that class; all subjects included. Actually, many professional course related educators have been doing that for years. Their programs have measurable objectives and standards that must be demonstrated by evaluation in order for the student to continue in the program. Unfortunately, accountability for what *all* the students should have learned is not part of the current teaching employment system. Take note that the current system, because of lecture-telling (Hearing and reading) caters to only those learners who more naturally absorb enough information heard and remembered from the lecturer to pass informational tests on the lecture and move on easier in the system. This selective teaching practice (lecture-telling) is deceptively justified by the use of statistical sampling whereby the student's test scores are analyzed on a graphically shaped Bell Curve (example: graphically plotting the test scoring range horizontally versus the number of students attaining those scores vertically). The deception is the inference drawn from the scores. The high scores are inferred to represent high student effort/learning and the low scores, unjustifiably and unfortunately, just the opposite. **In reality, the grades more logically represent the varying strengths of individual students' modes of learning: Hearing, Seeing, and Doing.** Those few whose natural receptive learning mode for lecture telling is very strong will tend to be at the positive tail of the curve (high grades) whereas those few with very poor receptivity to lecture, more naturally receptive to the other modes, will tend to be at the negative tail of the curve (low grades). The larger remaining group (varying and less biased modes of learning) appear in the center top and both descending sides of a resultant bell-shaped curve. In reality, this deceptive process of grade interpretation appears to justify low grades by relating them to low effort/learning; thus the failure of those who do not naturally learn well from lecturing (Hearing—listening and reading) which, as described previously in this Guide, includes a huge number of people.

TEACHING VERSUS TRAINING

Traditional Teaching (Hearing and reading) is more academic and knowledge based, theoretical and abstract; versus Training (Seeing and Doing) which is hands on practical and is perceived as adding skills onto existing knowledge.

This traditional accepted view of these two distinct types of education is now forcibly altered by the digital informational age. Today, academic subjects, out of necessity, have to be taught with both theoretical knowledge and application skills together. From the liberal arts, professional, and technical education, the subjects include varying levels of abstract mathematics, science, language, etc. *and the necessary application of those abstract concepts.* The distinction between Teaching and Training is now blended because of the necessity to understand the theoretical concepts as well as perform their use. Students, instead of just memorizing for the test, now ask Why? and How? and expect to see some relevance to what they learn. Educators have to develop the skills to interest the students in the applications of the knowledge they are teaching. Without teaching that promotes self- interest student attention span is reduced to nil and so is learning.

Teaching must include the learning methods of Seeing and Doing. Knowledge is perceived by the educational consumer to be dead-end without the ability to apply it.

Successful learning includes knowing that you know something by being able to use it. This reality, the general educational consumer needing the application skills for information age knowledge, is promoting an evolution in traditional Teaching versus Training by combining the learning modes of Hearing, Seeing, and Doing.

THE RESULT OF IMPROVEMENT

When a teacher plans and teaches using all the learning receptivity modes including Hearing (listening— reading), Seeing (observing reality), Doing (application—feeling) the intent that all their students must learn; the results tend to nullify the aforementioned curve, the grading inferences, and the justification for selective teaching by verbal lecture and descriptive reading. It is teaching directed to all students by utilizing all of the most common learning receptivity modes to acquire knowledge. The only variables remaining are the differences in the individual levels of information retention; they all were able to receive and process the information, but retained it at different levels. Logically the graded scores would be higher because more students receive/ process the information; **thus—more learn easier.**

Traditional Expectations

Example: An administrator reviewed a class grade sheet at the end of the semester and asked why the teacher had no failures, with the expectation that there should have been some. The teacher told him/her the way he/she taught was to ensure all students learned the information at an acceptable level, as documented by measured course objectives, and thus no failures. The teacher nullified the curve by teaching to each student's mode of learning, ensuring their receptivity of the required subject matter and that was reflected in the evaluation results and subsequent grades. The administrator did not question the answer but the teacher could tell that the administrator was disturbed by it and that only reinforces the argument as to the accepted structure of a system that is ill equipped to accept the notion that the only failure in the classroom is the teacher.

Remember, "Bell Curve" reported learning all goes back to the current teaching method which is most generally verbal lecture and descriptive reading. In actuality, the students are being graded on only how well they adapted to the verbal lecturing (Hearing and reading) and those that do not are eliminated from the system by low grades, dropping out, or staying out. If the overall effectiveness of lecture-telling is questionable, remember "I told him/her not to do it but they just didn't listen," then what about the evaluation stemming from that, and the advisement, and so on?

Years later those eliminated from the system tend to come back and do very well, many in similar classrooms, and the rhetoric/justification is they are "More mature now." More accurately they were disinterested because of inefficient learning (not on their wavelength); resultantly the topics did not make sense, they didn't understand/retain it, and because of all that they were perceived as poor students. The reality is that those students are usually the students who return to school after being in the world of work, finding they can learn by converting on-the-job "Hearing" information into Seeing and Doing applications at work and because they were successful, why can't they go back to school and do well in spite of their prior experiences?

The following chapters will begin examining the changes needed to improve learning and make the U.S. a world leader in education. When a student leaves school they find out quickly that for most employment in our society they are held accountable for their performance. Education resulting in poor student learning should not purposefully occur in a system accountable to the public. It is time to start making the instructional changes to establish a system on continuously improving student learning as the foremost goal.

Traditional Error In Learning Reinforcement

To teach more effectively to all students, utilizing all three modes of learning receptivity, requires continuous analysis and methodology improvement. Because this is not an instructional responsibility it sparingly occurs and the practice is to assign traditional type student homework as learning reinforcement. In reality, the homework is generally nothing more than the same verbal learning mode of teaching (students hearing themselves read) emphasizing the practice that more verbal learning is better for *all*. This practice is only positive reinforcement to those biased towards the Hearing mode of learning receptivity but conceptually in error by actually promoting negative learning reinforcement to those more receptive to the Seeing and Doing modes. Because the homework is not on their "wavelength" (even more difficult to learn at home than in class) those not as receptive to the Hearing mode struggle and become much more perceptively discouraged and disinterested, thus they drop-out or survive with low grades and become a stay-out. This is where the teacher "fails" the student. Not meaning the student receives an "F," although that may be a subsequent consequence.

> Teaching incorporating all three modes of learning for all course objectives should be a religious part of classroom instruction and is an instructional responsibility.

A reality is that those stay-outs who learned to adapt to the current system, in spite of the aforementioned deficiencies, have displayed and proven an exceptionally strong commitment to want to learn. Who is the real failure in their classroom?

> Exemplary Teachers tend to set the example that the only failure in the classroom is the Teacher.

IMPROVEMENTS

- Teach by ethically utilizing all three modes of learning receptivity for all course objectives.
- Measure, grade, and analyze student learning thus documenting teaching effectiveness.
- Teachers and administrators accept responsibility and accountability for analyzing student learning to document continuous improvement of instruction.

Notes:

Chapter 2: Methods for Learning

"He who knows and knows that he knows is a wise man—follow him;" Confucius, the *Analects*

To the Reader: Apply the following methods for "How to Improve Student learning" that will improve your teaching methodologies.

How We Learn

To ensure learning, educators have to begin by asking and answering the age-old questions: How do we know something? How do we know we know something? How do we learn?

The following is a method, similar to that used in private business teaching programs, to describe how people receive and begin to process information. To start: Please think about the following statement you are about to read, then analyze the statement and put yourself mentally in the particular situation that the statement refers to. Here is the Statement:

"Remember the last time you were at the beach or the ocean."

Now examine the way you processed this thought. If you processed this information visually you probably saw a picture of the beach or ocean in your mind. If you did it through auditory you might have heard the waves etc. If you did it kinesthetically (feeling) you might have felt the hot sun. You may have also used a combination of these modes.

The following are typical conclusions: The strong majority of people received and processed the information visually; typically because we have been receiving and processing information visually many more generations than we have been reading or concentrating on language interpretation. Biologically our physical system is more perfected towards visual information reception and interpretation. As such, the kinesthetic (feeling) mode would logically rank a biological second, and auditory (hearing) third. Now, what is the mode most often used in teaching? Unfortunately, auditory which is comparatively inefficient in information receptivity. Also, the following phrase relating to the auditory/reading teaching mode has become habit forming: "There is just no other way of doing it." In reality there is, it just requires planning new teaching methodologies to meet the receptive learning mode biases of *all* students.

LEARNING RECEPTION AND RETENTION

What process does a learner go through to not only put something into their mind, but then recall it from their mind, and then apply what is recalled? It would appear the whole notion of "learning" would have to include the aforementioned; putting something into one's mind, recalling it, and then applying it. One's varying ability to do that would then reflect a level of learning.

The most accepted research on learning says people put information into their minds by various combinations of Seeing, Feeling, and/or Hearing it. Although just seeing, feeling, and hearing information does not in itself totally constitute learning. These are only the most common modes people use to communicate information into their, and/or others, minds. It is also accepted in teaching practice that if learners actually apply the information they heard, saw, and/or felt, they would tend to remember it better; meaning they could recall and apply it when needed, thus learned it. It would be reasonable to deduce the more times learners applied the same information they heard, saw, and or felt, they would have learned it to a greater level.

The first important point in observing learning is to examine how educators go about communicating information to the learners. The norm seems to be to tell it by verbal instruction (expounding, urging, telling) identified in this Guide as lecture-telling. This appears to only justify one mode of learning—Hearing. The Seeing mode is intended to be justified by visually demonstrating something related to the topic. In education, this is traditionally implemented by using different media mechanisms such as a white board, computer screen, etc. Unfortunately, these mechanisms really represent the Hearing mode; the learners are repeating to themselves what they are reading from the board or computer and thus Hear themselves. The Feeling mode is traditionally left out of most teaching with the justification: "It does not relate well to general education subjects except for writing." Unfortunately writing is about as ineffective a representation of Feeling as the whiteboard is to the receptive mode of Seeing. Thus, the nature of the teaching-learning problem in our public education system.

Remember that Seeing, Feeling, and Hearing are the most common modes used to enter information into our minds. We also know people naturally receive and process information at different levels of reception via the three modes. Some do well with Seeing, versus others who do better with Feeling, versus others with Hearing, even though individuals tend to use one to all three abilities combined. However, these receptive modes can change in priority given the situation. People tend to receive information in reaction to the way it was sent. **As an example only:** A person holding their hand close to a warm stove will receive the information immediately through the Feeling mode even though they may be Hearing mode biased. In addition, a person's frantic motions received through the Seeing mode may take precedence over a Feeling bias. Overall people tend to use all three modes to receive and process information although individually have differing, and in some cases significant, personal biases utilizing those modes.

Traditional Learning Dilemma

A learning dilemma is created in the classroom when mainly using the lecture-telling (Hearing) instructional methodology. A learner who is more biased in the Seeing or Feeling modes of information reception naturally creates mental pictures or feelings of the verbal statements made by the teacher. As the telling continues the biased learner is concentrating on the mental pictures or feelings and is attentively missing some of the remaining telling, creating a dilemma. The dilemma is between the mental pictures and/or the verbal information—not retaining both at the same time. Explanation: "Neurological science has demonstrated that the human brain is incapable of focusing on two things at once." Naturally creating mental pictures or feelings in one's mind from lecture-telling sentences diverts from retaining subsequent verbiage thus the biased learner is prone to missing information. It is apparent that those biased learners suffer the consequence of receiving and processing information differently when only sent verbally thus creating a receptive distraction and uncertain learning.

This situation means that a large number of students will not escape their biological tendency towards receiving and retaining information through Seeing and Feeling and are subject to the dilemma created by lecture-telling. *Their learning will tend to be inversely proportional to the strength of their bias.* This receptive diversion affects so many learners/students and could be drastically resolved by teaching to the way students learn—making learning easier rather than more difficult.

Classroom experience (verbal lecture-Bell Curve) verifies that the number of significantly verbally biased learners tends to be small (positive tail of curve) which indicates that the larger number of remaining learners will be affected by the Traditional Learning Dilemma. Knowing this reality should motivate a conscientious teacher to improve their teaching methodologies.

> It is only logical that learners would receive and retain information more effectively if all three modes were used to send it. That is an important basis for effective instruction. In other words, teachers can reach more students, more effectively, utilizing all three modes.

Chapter 2: Methods for Learning

The learning dilemma is additionally exacerbated by the deceptive notion of success, when using the verbal lecture (Hearing) method alone. This is justified by the traditional interpretation of test grades that plot a Bell-shaped curve thereby documenting an accepted learning variance within the class *(traditionally acceptable to have low grades and failures)*.

Contrary to the acceptance of this variance is that those learners with the stronger receptive modes of Seeing and Feeling are in trouble right from the start. They are the learners who tend to return to school after being in the world of work, finding they can learn by using the other modes of Seeing and Feeling; and because they were successful, why can't they go back to school and do well, in spite of their prior teachers? Many do, and tend to do it very well.

In explanation: It is apparent that the Seeing and Feeling biased learners have significantly experienced converting on-the-job Hearing information into Seeing and Feeling (Doing) applications at work and thus were more successful learning (putting information into their mind, recalling, and applying it) than they ever were at school. *They actually wound up doing the job the formal teacher should have done.*

Learning with the Learning Dilemma

In traditional education those learners who have learning mode biases more related to Seeing and Doing versus Hearing have to reinforce their learning by recalling the missed information through notes, reading, discussion, and then study the missed information in order to gain a better understanding (learning). The learners separate the information and review it in their minds by reading or listening—trying to visualize it (Seeing) and/or visualizing the application of it (Doing) for memory retention. Thus, conversional learning takes additional time and makes learning more difficult. In addition, learning is very contingent on one's interest in the subject. The more interested the more motivated to conversional learning—and the converse. With little interest the learners tend not to focus on conversional learning but instead they tend to memorize it just for the Test. Thus, the learner "only knows" the information.

By teaching to the way all students learn, utilizing all the modes of learning, learning is made easier for all and the grading reflects higher information retention.

In review: Utilizing the lecture learning method alone forces the strong majority of students in the class to mentally convert the lecture material to their individual biases in order to understand or learn what is being taught. The students have to adjust their learning from the way the teacher teaches. It behooves the teacher to teach to the way the students learn thereby avoiding the additional mental conversions the students have to make in order to convert the material to their receptive wavelengths. They would learn the information easier.

The learning adjustments the students would have to make are also determined by their motivation—fueled by their interest. Without interest the biased learning mode students will forgo their effort in the conversion process and tend to test poorly.

Example: William, a young new math teacher, said his goal in teaching math was to take the class to the school laboratories and teach students math by showing how it is really derived and applied in real life. He said math fundamentals can and should be taught in the laboratories (applying all three receptive modes: Seeing, Feeling, and Hearing) where it is used. Incidentally, he meant real-life practical applications laboratories (art, industrial, music, etc.) which his school had, not the traditional math lab with only computers programmed to reinforce the telling methodology. William's intent coincided with the accepted educational theory that students can receive information more effectively utilizing the three modes—multivariate. Also remember, can receive information, not saying they would receive it. What is meant by that?

Today's learners appear to respond significantly different from yesterday's learners. The technology ease of making available large amounts of information has drastically changed the attention span of most people. If it interests them, they continue to read and or see on. If not, they hit mental delete and move on to the next item of initial interest. This conditioning directly relates to the learning behavior of the student in the classroom. If they are interested in the topic presented, and they are biased in the mode of presentation, they will probably do better than those disinterested will and/or biased otherwise. The real key here is if they are interested. If not interested, regardless of their learning mode bias, they will probably tend to tune out the presentation and focus some of their thoughts elsewhere, not able to receive and retain enough information to start the recall and application process of learning. Since the attention span of the learner today is so much shorter than that of previous years, it is necessary for the effective teacher to develop interest in the topic right from the start relative to any concepts and/or topics they are presenting.

Teaching, according to various dictionary definitions, is "to impart knowledge" and/or "to cause to learn." Unfortunately, that is how the traditional system has initiated learning problems; by only imparting knowledge through verbal lecture-telling, all interest aside, and if students remember it okay and if not—too bad. It is not uncommon for conventional educators to feel that their job responsibility is to present the information and the rest is up to the individual learner. If they recall it for the tests, then teachers assume they have learned it. Typical advice (unfortunate for those who are biased other than Hearing) is to read it, study it, go over it many times in your mind so you remember it for the test. In today's current world that does not work well. Attitude, time available, family structure, interest, environment, etc. are all affecting factors. To be an effective teacher one has the responsibility to impart knowledge in the most effective way, ultimately resulting in learning by the student. *Good teaching has to ensure learning.* If educators focus on ensuring learning they can resolve the problems currently plaguing us.

Example: Tom was a math teacher and every semester he would verbally expound to other faculty that he had too many students in his class so he would give extremely difficult assignments the first few class sessions until enough students dropped the course leaving him with fewer papers to correct and less responsibility. Tom did this every semester and had acceptable evaluations utilizing the same lecture-telling teaching methodology for every class resulting in scattered failures and/or letter grades of "D"—the justification given that the poorer students just "didn't do the work." Tom's personal effort was to reduce his class size and responsibility thus resultantly applying minimal effort to improve student learning. Tom, who had attained "continuous contract status" (tenure) was not held accountable for his student's grades, teaching methodology, or improvement of any kind. His reviews were minimal, procedural, and acceptable.

Whereas Virgil, another math teacher in the same school, had students waiting in line to take his course. Every semester he would refine and improve his teaching methodology until he was known throughout the school as being the best of the best. In reality he did not have to give low grades because his teaching methods were so diverse that he was able to reach all of his students and they knew it. Hard work and constant improvement made Virgil the best math related teacher in the school. His focus was always the improvement of student learning. Virgil was the example of successful "continuous improvement" and had adopted a personal responsibility improving student learning through improving his teaching—continuously. Virgil also had a continuous contract.

> The process of analysis and continuous improvement should be a definitive School employment requirement.

How to Ensure Learning

First: Develop an interest in the required topic. Find a way to show the learner how it will affect them in an important way.

One sentence as to the relevance of the topic doesn't work. Most people's attention is gained when the nature of the topic affects something important to them. Incidentally, threatening to give students an "F" grade does not promote interest and may actually promote the reverse. Topics necessary to be presented in classrooms or elsewhere generally have a beginning point. Someone discovered that knowledge somewhere and for some purpose of interest. Example: Where and/or Why did the subject of Algebra develop? Where and/or Why the Pythagorean Theorem? Where and/or Why does a minus times a minus equal a plus, etc.? These beginning points, Where and/or Why, are usually of interest to learners; **especially when related to how they seriously affect those learners today.**

Another reality is that many teachers are not aware of where/why/ or how those things were invented or developed. It behooves the teacher to know and present real interest in the topic in order to develop a reason to learn. People, even students, have to have a reason to want to do something. Learning something one sees no purpose in is a lost endeavor, defeated before starting, and much of today's verbal lecture without convincing purpose, is very successful at that.

Second: Teach all topics utilizing all three receptive modes: Seeing, Feeling, and Hearing. A lot of forethought, known as pre-preparation, will have to go into the design and implementation of this. The importance of this rule cannot be over stressed. Even if interested, if learners do not receive information on their wave-length many will be lost and/or experience greater difficulty in learning.

Example: The person who said their elementary grade teacher was having trouble with the students understanding the process of averaging numbers gave an example of the power of all three modes. In desperation, the teacher marched the whole class to the school gym where they had the final scores of all their school's basketball games posted on the wall. The subsequent teaching and learning is obvious—"Seeing" the actual scores posted, "Feeling" what it is like to be on the court where the scores actually occurred, and gaining a real life experience by actually manipulating (averaging) the score numbers viewed, where they occurred, in order to envision the future scores of their team. The important point here was twofold. The teacher engaged the students in all three modes of learning (teacher said he could see the light bulbs light up in the student's eyes) and the result was an adult who never forgot the experience, and the learning that took place because of it.

Another example was a freshman college class in Educational Psychology 101 where the teacher gave each student the option of attending the lecture class twice a week, or going to the local half-way house for four hours per week and report writing per course instructions. Who do you think learned more about educational psychology in that class? The students at the halfway house who were exposed to all three modes of learning, or those listening to the preached hearing mode only? See the value of the three modes of reception?

> Presenting information not utilizing the three receptive modes is ineffective because it restricts the natural learning opportunities of the student.

Third: Evaluate for recall and application of each measurable objective, then analyze and improve the instructional methodology utilizing all three improved modes. The evaluation after the teaching process is completed is not to grade the student, but to show the teacher what deficiencies exist in the methods of instruction. This gives the teacher the necessary opportunity to improve by analyzing and improving the subsequent re-teaching of those items for greater student learning; *all students in the class.* It serves as a teacher self-check and should be a necessary part of the teacher's continuous instructional improvement.

Fourth: Re-evaluate again for grading. The overall class results of the grading, personal name identification withheld, should be readily available information to be used for comparative improvement purposes. It is important for a teacher to develop the mental philosophy that the only failure in the classroom is the teacher. It is the teacher's job to ensure learning of the students. Effective teachers do take their responsibility personally. If students are failing in the class, then the teacher is failing. Look at all the great teachers in history. They all seem to follow the pattern of effective teaching previously outlined. They always developed interest in their various teachings which set the stage for learning. Their teachings were filled with Seeing and Feeling experiences, so much so that books thousands of years later still describe them. They even evaluated the applications of their student's learning in numerous ways.

In Schools and Colleges almost all extremely effective teachers have similar things in common. Their first concern is always student learning. Even the students know it; they feel it. They are hands-on, they most often develop instruction using the three modes, and their student evaluations of course objectives reflect their efforts. Few failures, if any, and always the highest perceived student evaluations. Their subjects even include Math and Chemistry, traditionally known for high levels of difficulty. Thus, in order to improve teaching and learning in America teachers must teach to continuously ensure learning and document it. Anything less is diminishing the students' opportunity to learn.

> The only failure in the classroom is the teacher.

CHAPTER 2: METHODS FOR LEARNING

TEACHER'S INFLUENCE ON LEARNERS

How to get students to learn? The applied psychology read, heard, seen, and actually experienced indicates that the practical answer to that question is to change ourselves. The reaction to our change tends to elicit a change in others. What is done, and how it is done motivates others, for the good or for the bad There does not appear to be a status quo in this; things are either going positive or negative all the time. People change to elicit a corresponding change in others and when that change disappears, they are back to the original situation.

Students are much more, or significantly more, perceptive than most educators ever give them credit for. They know and respond to the attitude, personality, and persona the teacher displays, consciously and/or unconsciously. Why is it that a seemingly small frail mature teacher can hold a class of 35 plus energetic high-school combined gender students spellbound and attentive versus the opposite person's physical stature, with opposite results? The students' perception of the teacher and their resultant behavior must be in reaction to whatever the teacher displays, does, or has done. A student's perception of non-verbal teacher characteristics is much more related to their classroom behavior (learning included) than one can imagine. If students perceive and believe teachers are concerned about their individual learning then their attitude towards accepting or learning what is being taught appears to be more instinctively motivated, or more positively influenced, This leads one to believe their level of learning will be greater. On the other hand, if a teacher is extremely effective in delivering the information being taught, but the students' perception of the teacher is threatening or impersonal, then the level of learning is decreased from what it could and/or should be.

The influence of the teacher's personal commitment to their individual learning, as perceived and believed by students, is one of the most learning related motivational factors in the classroom. This is overlooked and yet a significant factor relating to student learning. It is something very difficult to be taught for a teacher to do. It appears almost intrinsic to the character, personality, persona, and commitment of the person teaching. Excellent teachers have it. Maybe that is why many excellent teachers often appear to do their job in spite of financial issues—they love their job responsibility (student learning) and the students know, believe, and are motivated to learn because of it. This characteristic of excellent teachers is so common and would be difficult to be taught by any teacher education programs. Excellent teachers have it; others have to work harder to try to display/achieve it. Students, as well as others, react to what they See, Feel, and Hear—in that order. *Sound familiar?*

The continuous improvements in teaching methodologies that educators have to make is the subject of this Guide.

Chapter 2: Methods for Learning

It is not so much how excellent teachers are identified but the changes that have to be implemented to identify less effective teachers, continuously improve them; all to significantly improve student learning.

Improvements

- Create genuine student interest in all course objectives and abolish threats of any kind.
- Ethically incorporate all three receptive learning modes for teaching all course measurable objectives.
- Create intermittent course evaluations to measure student learning and evaluate teaching effectiveness of all major course objectives. Utilize the results for the improvement of instruction methodologies—continuously.
- Display a recognizable classroom attitude and demeanor that the teacher's primary priority is student learning.

Chapter 3 Reference: "The Impossibility of Focusing on Two Things at Once" MIT Sloan Management Review. Morela Hernandez

Notes:

Chapter 3: Responsibility and Accountability for Learning

It is a reality that holding the producer of a product accountable for the performance of the product ensures greater performance.

To the Reader: Apply the following improvements related to responsibility and accountability that will improve student learning.

Responsibility for Learning

It is logical to judge teaching, and the effectiveness of teaching, on the extent of student learning. It would be vague and misleading to conclude that the foremost responsibility of a teacher is just to "teach." In daily usage the verb "teach" has become more a figure of speech used to represent many differing perceptions, deflecting from its primary purpose; student learning. It is a reality that teaching purposefully causes student learning to take place therefore teachers are responsible for student learning. Unfortunately, one can teach and give instruction but that does not ensure student learning. This is the dilemma and challenge in traditional public education.

How is the verb "teach" defined? Dictionary examples include "to impart knowledge," "to bestow," "to give instruction," or more specifically, "to cause to learn." The real message in the definition of the verb "teach," is that something happens because of it; teachers are imparting, bestowing, giving, etc. *How are teachers imparting, bestowing, giving, etc., or how well are students learning?* What is the ultimate outcome of the process of teaching? It logically must be student learning. That is the very reason teachers are teaching; so students learn. Regrettably one can teach conventionally but if the students do not learn, the teaching effort is in vain. This Guide is written to remedy that challenge.

> A teacher's foremost responsibility is student learning.

Learning and Accountability

What does a teacher have to do to promote and ensure student learning? To begin, we have to ask and answer the question: learning of what? A necessary part of ensuring learning is that all major topics of instruction, therein to be learned, should be documented by some type of learning objective (result, aim, purpose, outcome, etc.) and a corresponding method of measuring student accomplishment of that objective. For the purpose of this Guide, the word "objective" is a noun and refers to that which is created by the teacher, and then is worked for to achieve. The definition of the word "goal" is for defining the overall purpose of a course of instruction. In essence, the overall course will have a goal, and subsequent to that, the informational topics necessary to reach that goal will be made up of cumulative objectives; measurable.

Measurable Objectives: How can one tell if the learners have met the topic objectives if the learning cannot be measured or if the objectives do not exist? If learner accomplishment of individual topic objectives cannot be measured, then one cannot document if learning of those objectives actually took place, at what level, and most important—the effectiveness of the teaching. Whatever topic is being taught, it should be derived, planned, and implemented with some type of measurable objective (result, aim, purpose, reason, outcome, etc.) and the evaluation results analyzed to document the effectiveness of the teaching. This analysis should be used as the basis for subsequent teaching improvements.

Typical objective questions regarding an educational institution's teaching effectiveness should include:
- What are the levels of effectiveness of teaching at your institution documented by class grade averages based on comprehensive

final evaluations or cumulative evaluations, grading all course objectives; all students, no exemptions?

- What is your institution's minimum acceptable level of teaching effectiveness, relative to student learning, as documented by class grade averages based on . . .?

The conventional response to instructional accountability is "Yes," the public is paying to learn but performance levels are confidential." Yet the public is aware that in the current world we can easily find evaluated performance levels of most products/services on the Internet before purchasing them. In public education, after the class is paid for and over, it is hidden. This makes the public wonder why and thus suspicious and critical.

Consider this: If the class comprehensive final evaluation grades, for all the students in the class, show half of the class received grades of C and above, and the other half received grades of C and below, that would indicate a lower level of student learning versus a similar class showing all C's and above. This process would reveal the level of learning that took place, relative to the course objectives, and thus the effectiveness of the teaching and necessity for improvement.

Concerned critics ask: What is the minimum acceptable level of teacher effectiveness for a class, relative to documented student learning, at your school/institution? Not sure? Educational institutions are always concerned about student learning but when it is tied to teacher effectiveness they tend to respond unknowing. Without documenting the effectiveness of teaching, there can be little accountability to the instructional responsibility of student learning. Little accountability reflects little improvement and/or complacency; this is the current reality.

To improve student learning it is necessary to document student learning, analyze the level of learning, and improve the teaching methodologies—continuously. Teachers must be able to show where they currently are, and then, where they are going. Doing this learning improves. Not doing this learning tends to stay the same, or regresses.

Learning with Measurable Objectives

For the most part, math, science, and other current world related courses appear to be "objectives" compliant; most often due to certification, registration, or other institutional, commercial, or standardized evaluation requirements. These entities, for the most part, require documentation of a student's performance.

Generally, during institutional accreditation review, courses and related instructional material do identify a course goal and then define varied general objectives to meet that goal. Examples of student performance (generalized testing) are usually provided to the reviewer with other course related materials. In the minimal of cases where strong documentation exists, verification of topic objectives and performance assessment of those objectives is mostly presented by educators who had significant experience in business, science, health, technology, engineering or other professional occupations before teaching.

The current challenge is that there is not an accountable method to promote this assurance of performance, for both teacher and student, other than a final course grade which in too many instances is derived from data far removed from actual measurable performance of course objectives. Think about it; if a teacher presents a topic and then assesses the learning of that topic, the outcome of the assessment not only documents the level of student learning, but also and more importantly, the effectiveness of the teaching. At that point, the teacher should determine what changes have to be made to increase student learning for that topic objective. The changes could require re-teaching the topic after improving the instructional methodology, etc. The important point being the teacher now knows how effective their teaching methodology was and now has the opportunity to determine what changes have to be made to assure an acceptable or increased level of student learning; for *all* students in the class. Conventionally, evaluation is viewed as a threat by students and is generally dismissed by teachers as an assessment of a teacher's effectiveness. The very nature and culture of this practice has to be improved in order to increase and assure student learning.

To be accountable for student learning the teacher should design, draft, and document all course major topics with written measurable objectives. Complimentary, the teacher should develop and document various ways to evaluate the student performance of those topic objectives. Unfortunately, many teachers take the easy way out and leave this task to the writers of related course texts and test questions at the end of the textbook chapters. Textbooks are written in specific readable format and should be used as the guide for the teacher's instructional methodologies but are not, and should not, be the course inclusive. To do this is to lose the advantage of individualized instruction; related text material developed and presented in a multi-mode format by a teacher who is familiar with the varying learning characteristics of the students in the class. The course topic objectives and the methods to teach and measure the accomplishment of those objectives should relate to the specific student group, in a person-to-person class setting.

Learning with Standardized Testing

Some state and national standardized testing requirements may persuade teachers to identify measurable objectives for all the major topics being taught in their course. This probably would occur out of a necessity to respond to whatever results are identified by standardized testing. If standardized test scores are low, the institution response may be "poor student performance" whereas the student/parent response may be "poor teaching." *In either case, the learning level of the students and the effectiveness of the teaching can and should be revealed by evaluating individual course objectives versus their corresponding class evaluation grades.* This review would identify what and where the learning problems exist and serve to justify planned improvement. If this documentation does not exist then the "disease cannot be identified and/or treated" and the patient (the student) permanently suffers (grades on transcripts do not disappear), and the problem only tends to repeat itself with a new group of students.

In review, the importance of standardized testing serves to not only identify student achievement, but also document teacher effectiveness. The resolution of poor student learning under the current operational and supervisory systems needs to be improved because it lacks an accountability process for analysis and continuous improvement. Without improvement the problems procrastinate and infect a completely new class by repeating themselves; and on and on. *Standardized testing can be helpful but standardized teaching would be, and is, contrary to the concept of continuous improvement.*

It is apparent that there are certain subjects/courses that relate to most curriculums of study and are natural candidates for comparative type testing. Therefore, it seems reasonable for educational systems to maintain similar course content in math, science, language, etc. Even the Greeks agreed on their "trivium" of lower division subjects (grammar, rhetoric, logic) thus demonstrating their educational common agreement. It cannot be ignored that as geographically widespread the U.S. educational system is, and as competitive as the individual systems have become, there should be some commonality in basic courses; thus the outcomes of those common courses would necessitate documented accountability. The learning challenge in the U.S. is not Standardized Testing; it is improving student learning to achieve the standardized outcomes tested.

If we, as a nation, want to be a leader in world education then we have to promote improvement in student learning. This will be accomplished through a process of analyzing student learning, then improving teaching methodologies—continuously.

Developing the Interest to Learn

What does the teacher have to do to promote student learning? In addition to creating the learning objectives for individual courses, and the methods of evaluating and documenting the student learning of those objectives, it is a fundamental responsibility of the teacher to generate "the cause to learn." Necessity is the mother of invention;

without establishing and convincing students of the necessity of learning the individual objectives it will be that much more difficult for learning to take place. People do what they tend to be interested in; if the teacher does not or cannot develop student interest in the subject matter of the topic objectives, one cannot expect students to learn just because they are told about it, or told to do it. This is one of the greatest challenges the teacher faces: determining how the individual course topic objectives meaningfully relate to the students. If a student is convinced the information presented is needed, then real learning tends to take place. If the student cannot see the need or necessity in the information, they either memorize it or just plain let it go out of the memory window. Overall, it has long been accepted there is a strong correlation between interest and learning. The teacher must develop "necessity interest" in the student if improved learning is to take place.

Example: (A rare exception when motivation to learn exceeded what was needed): A faculty member who parked daily at the Newman Center (college campus religious support organization) was dramatically surprised when he went to put a working TV into the Newman Center donation dumpster. As he went to put the TV into the dumpster a voice screamed inside the dumpster pleading not to put anything in his sleeping area. Upon investigation a student had been *illegally* sleeping in the donation dumpster at nights, showered in the gym during the days, studied in the library, all to save living costs so he would have minimal debt when he graduated. When the temperature got too cold (campus was in warmer southwest U.S.) the student would use the couch in the Newman Center although he said his preference was the dumpster. The student, who was close to graduation, was adamant about not owing anyone money when he graduated, and supported himself with a part-time job to pay for his basic educational costs.

The faculty member was shocked and left the parking lot wondering if what he had just experienced really happened. Again, there is probably a lot more to this story then related here but the motivation of the student could not be dismissed. *This example of a real-life illegal incident is not recommended by the author, not allowed by campus rules, and compliance is enforced by campus security.* This example describes the unrealistic lengths that a student might attempt in order to accomplish a desired goal—when self-motivated.

Contrary to self-motivation, how many readers of this text have sat in classes at either the elementary, secondary (high-school), or college level and wondered why they were even there? Unfortunately, some whole courses are this way and they persist semester after semester. Years later, generally in the world of work, some significant happening will trigger the memory flash of that boring teacher and class with the wonderment of why the teacher did not use what just happened as an example to generate interest. Too little class preparation, too late, too little experience, or possibly the teacher just lectured and was not really interested in multi-mode student learning. This type of teaching is what educators will have to significantly improve in order to be the world's leader in education.

Learner Performance and Learning Improvement

In practice new teachers, those just entering the profession, tend to take more time to investigate interests and motivate their students even though they may not have significant experience in the course material. They are extremely interested in what they are doing and the impact they will make. Additionally, those new teachers, who have spent a number of years in the world of work before beginning the profession of teaching, have the advantage of experiencing real life applications of the course material and find it easier to promote student interest; convincing others of why it is important. Those professional teachers in the middle group seem to be split into two groups. Those that can create such student interest you can hear a pin drop in their class. There are "general education" teachers like this who, on occasion, have extra un-enrolled students sitting in the aisle space of their classroom just to See, Feel, and Hear the topical information with their class enrolled friends because it was presented multi-mode, and thus so interesting. Then, there's the other type of teacher, who was just doing enough of their job to escape the wrath of a litany of complaints. All of the above situations would be clearly documented by evaluating learner performance of individual course topic objectives to determine the level of learning and thus the effectiveness of the teaching. This should then be analyzed by the faculty member continuously and changes made in the methods of instruction to improve the level of student learning for *all* students in the class.

Complimenting the Use of Textbooks

Traditionally textbooks are the accepted source of "how to." For the most part, the authors have extensive knowledge of the material they are presenting in the text, but many times that can be a detriment instead of a help. For instance, there's the author who too briefly emphasizes the importance or application and focuses the majority of the written material on the concept itself. This is not necessarily bad, however many times it is minimally useful in the interest promotion process. Too often experts in their field write the texts used in courses and spend most of the text on the mechanics of whatever they are presenting. Introductory paragraphs or explanations rarely explain sufficiently and convincingly why and how this affects the reader. Therefore, it does little to generate reader interest.

The experts are so focused on the mechanics of the presentation, which rightfully is of great interest to them, that the basic motivation is generally thought to be expected rather than needed to be generated. This is where the teacher must compliment the text and not ignore what seems academic to them. The writers of course texts have an extreme interest in the subject because it interests them. Such may not be the case for new learners/readers and must be significantly reinforced by the teacher. This, again, is part of course planning and takes time to develop, which is probably why it is not as common a practice as it should be.

> Generating student interest is the foremost promotion of learning that a teacher can make. There are few things more important in the responsibilities of the teacher than instilling a believable need to learn the material presented.

Responsibility and Accountability

If the responsibility and accountability for student learning is dependent on teaching then schools and colleges can logically expect to get a greater overall commitment to classroom learning. The converse is also true and is a major part of the challenge preventing the U.S. from becoming the foremost leader in education in the world. Clear thinking indicates that people cannot solve problems if they don't know what they are. A perceived necessity for any improvement is truly the mother of invention in government, business, or an educational classroom. If people have to they will generally find a way to improve. If they do not have to, especially when due to a lack of accountability and continuous improvement, then complacency breeds. The unfortunate part is the student ultimately carries the consequence of complacency; poor learning. Educators, leaders, etc., are logically responsible and accountable for what they produce. "It is a reality that holding the producer of a product accountable for the performance of the product ensures greater performance."

Improvements

- Create measurable objectives for all major course topics.
- Inspire student motivation and generate a cause to learn for all course topics.
- Teach by ethically utilizing all three modes of learning receptivity for all course objectives.
- Document a "class grade average," evaluating and grading the level of learning of all course

measurable objectives and resultant teaching effectiveness, for each assigned course.

- Compute the "class grade average," using comprehensive final evaluation grades or cumulative evaluation grades; for all enrolled students, no exemptions.
- Prepare a continuous teaching improvement plan by analyzing the range and dispersion of evaluation grades for individual topic objectives—versus improved methods of instruction.

Notes:

Notes:

Chapter 4: Preparation for Student Learning

Preparation is the most important step in teaching. If preparation is inadequate the results will be poor levels of learning characterized by a number of disruptive classroom situations.

To the Reader: Apply the following improvements related to preparation that will improve student learning

The Learning Plan

IN PUBLIC EDUCATION (TRADITIONAL) THE emphasis is on teaching: expecting students to learn the way the teacher teaches; emphasizing the verbal learning mode (Hearing and reading).

Outside of public education (proprietary/business) the emphasis is on learning: expecting teachers to teach the way students learn; emphasizing multi-learning modes (Seeing, Doing, and Hearing). This is proven more effective in improving student learning but requires thorough pre-preparation and planning.

Successful people plan their work; then work their plan. Thus, to teach effectively would necessitate the pre-preparation and development of a plan, a Learning Plan. This one-page plan, concentrating specifically on ensuring student learning, should consist of the following four headings/elements:

- Topic Objective,
- Methodologies for Learning,
- Analysis of Learning,
- Improved Methodologies.

This plan, limited to one page, is essential to continuously improve student learning and is described as follows:

Topic Objective

The first step in preparation is to divide the course or lesson information into topic objectives. The most important information to be learned should be represented by stated/written objectives; the reason for teaching the topic. Call it what whatever: objectives, results, aims, purposes, reasons, etc. The knowledge to be learned should be represented by a statement describing the resulting expectations of what is being taught. More importantly, what the learner should be able to do as a result of the methodologies used.

Example: At the end of this (lesson, session, topic, etc.) the learner should be able to correctly (perform, complete, compute, solve, etc.)…the actual purchase price of a discounted item given the various methods of store discounting without the use of a calculator.

Example: As a result of this... the learner should be able to accurately interpret the author's meanings...

Example: At the end of this... the learner should be able to correctly solve a problem containing ...

Example: As a result of this... the learner should be able to both accurately investigate and verbally communicate the...

These examples should state the objective of the teaching; what the learner should be able to know and perform as a result of the teaching effort. It is the necessary basis for the remaining preparation including: Methodologies for Learning, Analysis of Learning, and Improved Methodologies. It is the most important step in preparation of teaching. It is the necessary starting point; describing what the learner should be able to do—the expected result.

The entire course or body of knowledge that the teacher is responsible for will have to be represented by these objectives. This means thoroughly pre-reviewing the course or lesson content and writing the objectives. When written, the topic objectives represent the initial pre-planned stepped outcomes of the course. This is necessary to ensure the planning, implementation, and analysis of student learning. Without topic objectives, teaching to ensure learning and subsequent continuous improvement will be next to impossible to document and achieve. Therefore, each topic objective should be recorded as the first statement in the teacher's one page learning plan. This is the written/

formatted outline for that particular teaching session thus the course will be made up of cumulative one page learning plans.

In review: the learning plan is a comprehensive one-page document per objective and is a necessary teaching/learning working guide. It details what is to be learned, how to teach it, an analysis of learning, and subsequent improvements. It is the teacher's essential plan to ensure student learning and continuously improve. So now, the first essential statement in the learning plan is the Topic Objective.

Note that the lesson material itself (actual information to be taught and learned) is separate from the learning plan and can take traditional forms such as text books, notes, documents, etc., from which the objectives are derived.

METHODOLOGIES FOR LEARNING

It is the preparation of the Methodologies for Learning that will determine how well the learners receive the information presented. Remember that individuals receive and process information via the three most common modes: Seeing, Feeling, and Hearing. If a teacher decides to only verbally teach then they are reaching those biased to Hearing and creating a learning dilemma for those receptive otherwise. To be on the receptive wavelength of all the students teachers must present the information utilizing all three modes. To do this requires that the one most familiar with the subject matter, the teacher, develop strategies to accomplish this. What is it that the teacher can ethically invent, develop, present, involve students in, etc. that compels the learner to not only hear, but to see and feel the subject matter effects of the topic being taught. Seeing would involve utilizing experiences from various traditional media methods to real life visual applications. Receiving information through feeling involves experiencing physical involvement, reactions, applications, movement, doing, etc. Examples of teaching methodologies involving all the modes of learning are around us in everyday life. One only has to ethically relate similar processes to the classroom. Whether a student is to learn a mathematical formula, chemical procedure, geographical term, language grammar, philosophical concept, poetry, etc., it is more effective to see the topic objective applied, in addition to actually applying it. This is essential to ensure learning.

Example: Students to bring to class (examples only) of items advertised to be purchased at whatever discount offered and use each item as examples to learn how to determine the actual purchase price etc. The students are involved in Seeing and Doing with example items as they learn solutions for: percentage discounts, two for one, buy one half off other, etc.

Another methodology example is in teaching the non-visual internal structure of a metallic material; an abstract/

theoretical subject. The lecture-telling scenario was to draw the internal molecular structure on the white board and verbally describe the physical changes (dimensions and hardness) of the structure versus temperature changes. Student testing always produced mixed levels of results. As part of analyzing the test grades, versus the topic objective, improvement in the teaching methodology was obvious and necessary in order to improve student learning. Thus a real-life demonstration of the actual effects of the molecular change in the material was developed.

Example: Actual metallic material is heated (safety precautions taken) to documented temperature levels and cooled both rapidly and/or slowly so the students could visually see and test the different physical changes (dimensions and hardness) in the material versus the different rates of cooling.

Almost every time that real-life demonstration was performed (to a class of 35 to 45 students) some student always yelled out appreciatively: "that's what my chemistry teacher meant." Ironically, many teachers were taught the same concept verbally and never really understood the concept until they experienced it in real life applications. Seeing the application of a concept is believing. The methodology was also extended by having students investigate examples of the concept application outside of the classroom and report back their findings. This represented the feeling mode of learning and was verified by almost

Chapter 4: Preparation for Student Learning

always 100 percent level of learning response to the testing of that topic objective; a significant improvement from prior learning of that objective.

The methodologies for learning developed by a teacher will be unique to each person teaching the topic assigned. A teacher's experience, knowledge, demeanor, etc. may dictate the way this is done. It should be developed for each objective, recorded as part of the learning plan, and continuously improved through analysis of the student's level of learning versus the related method of instruction. Again, this is a necessary part of the learning plan and is the part most essential to improvement. So, now the learning plan has two essentials: the Topic Objective and the Methodologies for Learning.

Example: An exemplary teacher, called Dr. Ed, said his greatest challenge was teaching math (concepts of addition, subtraction, multiplication, division) to a group of immigrants who lacked formal education. He said for learning to be more effective he eliminated the classroom lecture-telling (Hearing) methodology for this group and instead took them outside on the rear school lawn and, using the instructional multi-modes of Seeing and Doing, related those modes to learning mathematics by utilizing actual crop planting processes (something they could relate to because of their agriculture background). Yes they grew crops, learned math, and met the objectives of the course. Dr. Ed was elated *the level of learning was so high* in a group that no other faculty member wanted to even begin to teach. Imagine the planning that Dr. Ed had to do to relate the Seeing and Doing methods of instruction to the environment in order to successfully complete the math topic objectives of the course. Dr. Ed truly believed the only failure in the classroom was the teacher—he is genuinely missed. Thanks, Dr. Ed.

Analysis of Learning

To get to the point where you are reading this text one must realize that you have had experience in testing; if not as a teacher; certainly as a student. Therefore, most readers are familiar with written essay, computer formats, multiple choice, and practical applications as they are the most common experiences of the education survivor. An example: everybody sitting and responding by computer to multiple questions of lecture-telling is the very nature of conventionally testing verbal learning. Good for verbal learners; others not so good. Effective teachers have found that there are many other methods of evaluating the levels of learning and some actually involve learning while evaluating. **Example:** Giving portions of questions to small groups of students, made up from a large class, with the goal of having each small group work to verbally agree on answers to their assigned questions. Then, have each group present their answers verbally in the large class meeting until all

CHAPTER 4: PREPARATION FOR STUDENT LEARNING

groups were heard and involved in the derivation of those answers. After that learning experience evaluate for the level of learning of the topic objective.

The important point in evaluation is to determine how well (at what level) *all* the students learned the material utilizing the methodologies for learning, and then use that data to improve the methodologies for learning next time—continuously.

Analyzing the learning: The conventionally accepted graphical analysis of class grades is a Bell-shaped curve ranging from effective learning high scores to non-effective learning low scores. It is obvious to ensure learning of all students in the class that a curved graph and/or low scores indicates an immediate and necessary change in the methods of instruction—even to the point of re-teaching the topic objective.

> A teacher's goal, depicting student learning, should be a high range of grades, with minimal dispersion, representing the successful level of learning of that respective objective for all students in the class.

It is apparent that levels of learning, naturally due to variances in students, will change with each different class/

group, even when utilizing the same methods of instruction. This is reason enough to continually improve the teaching methodologies based on an analysis of learning of each topic objective. The real challenge of the teacher is not to try to change the students but to change the methodologies for learning which in turn will change the learning outcome of the students.

Even with the variance in student groups it seems reasonable to accept the concept that learning will improve with most teaching methodology improvements. This is readily apparent from analyzing grades, resulting from improvements in teaching methodologies (for individual topic objectives) evolved over many classes. To make improvements one time, based on student's levels of learning, is defeating the goal of continuous improvement and depriving the learners of the teacher's professional abilities. That is why this should be an on-going process, analyzing the evaluation results of student learning of the corresponding topic objective and then improving the methodologies for learning. This is not a onetime event but rather a continual process of improvement. This analysis and improvement should occur every time an individual topic objective is taught. If you are teaching to ensure learning you must analyze the learning and improve the instructional methodologies continuously. That is how a teacher becomes excellent at what they do. Without a continuous process of improvement natural complacency appears and student learning suffers the consequences that we as a nation currently exhibit: mediocre international ranking, low college admissions SAT scores, high drop-out rates, and disenchanted stay-outs.

Now the learning plan has three essentials: the Topic Objective, Methodologies for Learning, and an Analysis of Learning.

Improved Methodologies

The real challenge of the teacher is not to try to change the students, but to improve the methodologies for learning, which in turn will improve the level of learning of the students. This is the real-world proven concept of analysis and continuous improvement and appears to be standard practice for those perceived as excellent teachers.

Realistic examples of needed improvement are apparent when a topic objective is taught utilizing the verbal methodology only. Testing usually reveals who the better verbal learners are and those who are not. The grades achieved will make these distinctions readily apparent. Improving the teaching methodologies, utilizing all the multi-modes of Seeing, Feeling, and Hearing, should typically result in quite different learning and grading results. Instead of the grades being skewed in favor of the more natural verbal learners, the grades tend to portray a more uniform and higher level of student learning for all—more students learn easier and thus better.

In reality, the analysis of learning shows the teacher how effective the teaching methodologies were and thus is documented justification for planning new methodologies, continuously. Continuously—meaning the improved methods become the Methodologies for Learning the next time the topic objective is taught, and so on, thus continuous improvement for learning.

Another reason to document improved methodologies is related to one's teaching performance evaluation. Learning plans are documented examples of improvement and can serve to positively justify reappointment and/or continued employment. It not only says that "I am doing my job," but documents credible effort to continuously improve student learning; the most important responsibility of the teacher. It is hard to imagine a supervisor, school district, school board, parents, etc. not positively accepting the very nature of documented improvement, especially when evident and directly relative to improvement in student learning. One often hears the statement that "the best job insurance is to make yourself so valuable to your employer that they cannot afford to be without you." Under normal circumstances it is difficult to imagine an educational organization divesting itself of well documented effective teachers. Learning plans are an excellent investment in improving student learning as well as documenting professional performance. The very nature of successful improvement is derived from

Chapter 4: Preparation for Student Learning

the well proven axiom: "Plan your work first, then work your plan."

Now, the complete learning plan has four essentials: the Topic Objective, Methodologies for Learning, Analysis of Learning, and Improved Methodologies.

> The one-page learning plan is a working document. It is the teacher's guide to ensure and continuously improve student learning.

Example: The college department secretary announced to the academic department head that there was a student named John who wanted to file a complaint against a faculty member. The conversation began with the student displaying all of his test papers and graded assignments; all graded at the level of "A."

The concern of the student was that his final course grade was a "B" and that did not relate to all of his course graded work. When asked why the discrepancy the student said that the initial course description sheet said he could only miss two class sessions and any more would result in a reduction of the course grade. John said he had missed three sessions. The department head then questioned John if he understood the course requirements as outlined on the description sheet. John respectively said that he completely understood the requirement and that was not his complaint. His complaint was that the faculty member himself missed 4 class sessions with no substitute in his absence. Class attendance was recorded by a work-study student (employed by the school) even though the classes, including John's absences, did not officially/actually meet. Attendance was taken and then the students were dismissed. There was dead silence from the department head. Obviously. John's point was that the faculty member should be held to similar responsibilities as the students—more importantly, John was charged with absences for classes that did not actually meet and because of that his grade was reduced.

Unfortunately, the only alternative process for grade change available to this student was to refer the grade issue complaint to the student review committee, which John did, and the committee recommended a grade change to "A." Ultimately the faculty member refused the grade change so John was held to the lower grade.

To further compound the issue was the information about the class sessions which revealed that each student in the class was assigned a number of topics to investigate and verbally report on for 20 minutes each—4 different students reporting for an hour and a half class session. All the faculty member did was to monitor the verbal reports during each session for the whole semester.

This is an excellent example of minimal and non-accountable lesson preparation by an educator who was putting the burden of verbal teaching on the students in the class. There was no administrative review of the coursework for that subject because the faculty member was employed under a continuing contract (tenure) and supervision requiring change would have minimal effect. This was not a class related to communication skills but rather a specific course in a Major field of study that should have required a significantly greater depth of Major Field information and academic rigor. This type of issue would have been exposed and resolved under a process of "continuous improvement" whereby "Learning Plans" would be reviewable.

Focus on Learning

For many years educators have been focusing on just verbal teaching and descriptive reading, taking learning for granted. Now, due to low college admission scores, high drop-out rates, indeterminable number of stay-outs, and the increasing flow of students to alternative learning endeavors, it's time to significantly change what is being done. Now is the time to redirect the focus to learning and let the process of how students learn dictate how teachers teach, instead of the other way around.

In public education the emphasis has been on teaching, expecting all students to learn from the way the teacher teaches. This emphasizes lesson plans that focus on a single mode of learning (Hearing) through verbal lecture and reading; resulting in reward/penalty grading.

In proprietary education the emphasis is on learning, expecting teachers to teach the way students learn. This emphasizes learning plans that focus on the multi-modes of learning with analysis of learning for continuous improvement; the goal being higher and less diversity in grades and easier learning for all. This is how to improve student learning in schools and colleges.

> Educators should demonstrate their response to the rhetorical question: What bottom line benefits the educational consumer (the learner) the most: teaching or learning?

Improvements

- Divide all major course information into measurable topic objectives.
- Create a one-page Learning Plan for each objective stating: the Topic Objective, Methodologies for Learning, Analysis of Learning, and Improved Methodologies.
- Create multi-mode methodologies for learning for each topic objective.

- Analyze learning (analyze the range and dispersion of evaluated grades) for all topic objectives
- Continuously amend/improve the learning plan's Improved Methodologies based on the analysis of learning, each time a topic objective is taught.

Notes:

Chapter 5: Evaluation of Students

The most important purpose of student evaluation is improvement of instruction.

To the Reader: Apply the following improvements related to the evaluation of students that will improve student learning.

Evaluation

EVALUATING STUDENT LEARNING IS THE only logical way a teacher can determine the effectiveness of their teaching. How well have the students learned the material presented by the teacher? Knowing this is necessary to plan teaching methodologies that will be more effective for the group being taught. The methodologies can and probably will change from group to group (class to class) but the necessity of multi-mode teaching versus single mode teaching still remains in order to improve student learning. People (students) receive and process information utilizing all three modes of learning, each to their individual mode biases. Some are better receiving information through Hearing, some Seeing, some by Doing, yet all tend to use all the modes at differing levels (depending on their interest) therefore all three are needed to be most effective in group (classroom) learning. A very astute educator once quipped: "the variances in the different modes of student learning, and the interest of the individual student at the time of learning, is likened to a dice game aboard the deck of an aircraft carrier during a typhoon." Things change all the time and the best way to prepare for the changing individual modes of learning is to present learning material multi-mode—continuously.

Given the variances in learning modes it would appear necessary to evaluate student learning utilizing the various modes although that may not be practical in large classes or time constraints. Evaluation via written answers, checked off multiple choice, etc. evaluates the verbal mode of learning and might appear questionable for evaluating the other multi-modes because the student has to convert the other modes of learned information to a verbal test answer. This may not be as difficult as it appears because the learning has already taken place, using multi-modes, and only needs to be converted mentally to answer written questions. The teacher should be able to verbally evaluate the level of learning of all the multi-modes used in learning the material. The goal of evaluation is to determine the level of learning of the teaching methodologies used— so a verbal and/or a multi-mode evaluation process should accomplish that.

Chapter 5: Evaluation of Students

Methods of Evaluation

What can the teacher devise to evaluate their student's learning of the material, or whatever, that was presented. If the learning was for verbal communication then the evaluation should be similar—even when all three modes of learning were used. If a mathematical computation, then the assessment should relate to the actual use of the computation in real applications—not just the written/computer completion of an equation—but more so the application of the equation. If a science project or concept, then the application of the concept rather than the verbal definition, etc. All of the above assessments (evaluations) would be a more realistic evaluation of instruction when related to the applications of the concept taught—not just the mechanics, although an understanding of how whatever is derived is essential. This is really evaluating the purposeful outcome of teaching, whatever is being taught. The actual evaluation method could be an individual assignment format, a group problem/solution format— something that puts the learner in the position of having to correctly apply the multi-mode information received from the teacher.

A paper/pencil/computer test is perceived to accurately assess the student's ability to respond to verbal information retained by all the students. Because most of the students in a class have differing receptive learning biases it would appear to be an inaccurate measure of student learning of the total class, even a class that was taught multi-mode. However, students do convert multi-mode learning to verbal responses based on their memory and interest. Contrarily, if the class was only taught verbally then the traditional student assessment of learning does not relate to multi-mode learners and would appear to be an ineffective measure of learning for that group.

One can see how important it is to teach and assess multi-mode learning for continuous improvement of instruction. Without multi-mode teaching the teacher will never know the comprehensive learning level capabilities of the student group, or individuals, thus the effectiveness of the teaching. Multi-mode teaching is most effective but multi-mode testing is not always practical. In many situations verbal testing is the only alternative and should produce evaluations that are accurate enough to determine the level of student learning which then can be used for improving teaching methodologies.

> The purpose of evaluating students is to improve instruction.

Student Grading

Traditional forms of student grading include:
- Letter grades of: S and N: S (satisfactory), N (needs improvement)
- Letter grades of: O,S,N: O (outstanding), S (satisfactory), N (needs improvement)
- Letter grades of A,B,C,D,F: A (outstanding), B (above average), C (average), D (below average), F (failing).

A typical percentage system for the letter grades of A through F is: A 90-100%, B 80-89%, C 70-79%, D 60-69%, F less than 60%. There are numerous grading systems used in school systems in the U.S. to designate A through F grades but all are similar in nature to the one described here. Variances most often occur in the percentages assigned to each letter grade.

Sometimes a letter grade of "I" indicates an Incomplete which has individual school rules for converting to a letter Grade. Usually, if not converted within an established time, the "I" grade automatically converts to an F grade.

Letter grading is in common use in the U.S. school system and portrays the student's level of learning of whatever subject/objective it represents. In reality it portrays the level of learning of the student per the given instruction of the teacher (methodology). Differing modes of instruction versus differing modes of student learning will produce varied results, given the same learning objective. That is why student evaluation will really indicate the effectiveness of the instruction and serves as the basis for methodology improvement.

Example: An elementary school had adopted the "O, S, N" grading policy and during a teacher's conference, with a student's parents, the teacher was asked why the parent's child could not receive a letter grade O on her work. They indicated their 2nd grade child was frustrated in that she worked so hard to submit assignments that were correct but was never able to receive an O grade. The teacher quickly responded by saying: "there is no kid worth an O." The parent was stunned. The teacher continued: "I do not give out O's." It was the teacher's discretion to apply grades and she felt none of her students were worth O grades so she just gave the grades of S or N. The grade of O was not attainable. The parent was taken back by the attitude of the teacher and the consequence that the child no longer wanted to go to school.

This teacher's grading process was contrary to creating the incentive to work towards the reward of a higher grade. Had the teacher evaluated the level of learning of the assignments or tests, and made instructional improvements continuously, the level of learning and grading would have increased.

It is questionable that a professional teacher would develop such a grading bias—which was reinforced by being a continuous contract (tenured) faculty member. The school had the normal faculty evaluation processes in place that lauded the performance of the teacher, irrespective of parental concerns.

Curve Grading

Grading on a curve is the process of adjusting test scores in order to ensure a selected grade distribution throughout the class. The actual test scores are adjusted to obtain a desired distribution of grades (generally known as a normal distribution or a normal curve). In explanation: "The curve" refers to a Bell shaped curve, recorded on a graph that all student scores are desired to resemble when plotted. The test scoring range is horizontal and the number of students attaining those scores vertical. The expectation is: few A's, some B's, many C's, Some D's, and few F's—thus a Bell shaped curve.

An example is distributing 15 percent of whatever the class scores for an A grade, 20 percent for a B grade, 30 percent for a C, and so on. The expectation here is that actual grades are spread out (the grading distribution is pre-determined) to assign grades A's through F's). No matter what the actual test scores are, the grades assigned will be pre-determined by the selected distribution. This grading procedure is *not* useful for continuous improvement because it does not portray the actual level of learning of the objectives tested for each of the students in the class. The effectiveness of the teaching has to be determined by the actual level of learning of the students.

Example: A student was discussing the results of a test that was taken in a college upper division course (3rd and 4th year). The teacher was new to the school, and teaching, and used the curve grading system. The student indicated that the test was to be on topics presented in class in the prior weeks. In actuality the test covered numerous required topics that were never covered in class (nor separately assigned) and as a result the highest score recorded in the class was approximately 40%. The teacher awarded the 40% a letter grade of A. The student who was discussing the results of the test only received a 20% score but was recorded as a B or C grade. In reality the class evaluation of the material learned was recorded with grades that seemed normal (grade distribution) when actually the level of learning was so low the test never should have been given because the students had little knowledge of the material required. As this was a course in a Major field of study the students never learned the material they were responsible for, *the grades indicated the opposite,* and the teacher's evaluation of instruction, based on student testing, was acceptable

Example: A lower division college course (1st and 2nd year) graded on a curve produced the following results. It was a course related to applied mathematics and required the application of trigonometry to solve problems. The teacher would give weekly tests and selected five problems from numerous problems given at the end of each chapter in the course textbook. A class of about 25 students knew this and decided to meet at night to work out the problems so everyone understood how to solve and show their work of the solutions. The teacher was a "curve grader" and would not allow asking questions or receiving answers on homework during class. The next day the class took the test and the result was a "perception of learning disaster:" The whole class received a grade of 100 percent except for one person who had misplaced a decimal point one decimal place, on a minor calculation on one of the five problems. Because of that, and the grading on the curve process, the student failed the test and was given the grade of "F" even though the remainder of his test answers were all 100 percent correct. The "perception of education" damage to the student who received the "F" was distinct. The result was to promote more "stay-outs." Many military veterans were in the class and their perception of what happened was indescribable. In spite of complaints to administration, the F grade stood as assigned.

EVALUATION FOR IMPROVEMENT

Evaluating students for improvement of instruction can most efficiently be accomplished utilizing the A to F (non-curve) grading system. This easily lends itself to numerical comparisons of learning levels of objectives tested. The comparisons will indicate areas of teaching methodology improvements needed as well as current successes. Test results indicating a diverse spread of grades, A to F's, is a signal that the teaching methods are not reaching all the students. Some are getting it, and some are not, thus indicating a need for improvement in the teaching methodologies. Possibly more multi-mode or more interest, or whatever. The challenge of the teacher is to make the instructional changes that will produce a more straight-line graph plotting A to C rather than the curve which acknowledges, and thus promotes, below level and failure learning.

The goal of continuous improvement is that the learning in the whole class be represented by test results that appear skewed when plotted indicating A's to C's with minimal (none) down curve to D's and F's. Multi-mode teaching, reaching all the students, should effectively produce results that nullify the Bell Curve and document results of more effective learning for all in the class. Again, this is the challenge of becoming an effective teacher—to evaluate student learning and make the instructional changes that will improve learning, continuously. "The most important purpose of student evaluation is improvement of instruction."

In conclusion, it cannot be expected that every student will learn to high expectations when teaching to ensure learning through the process of continuous improvement, but logically learning would improve immeasurably over current methodologies and the perception of education would be less threatening, more inviting, and ultimately more effective. This is how to improve student learning.

Improvements

- Create student evaluations of course objectives when utilizing all three modes of learning.
- Grade all evaluations on a percentage grading scale to identify the level of learning of course objectives.
- Improve the methods of instruction based on the level of learning of course objectives identified in evaluations.
- Evaluate and improve the methods of instruction continuously.

Notes:

Chapter 6: Elimination of Gender Bias

Gender Bias can negatively influence student course selection and career decisions resulting in too many students not becoming all they are capable of being and/or interested in being.

To the Reader: Apply the following improvements to eliminate gender bias that will improve student learning.

Gender Bias

GENDER BIAS EXISTS IN MANY forms; in the home, school, and the workplace. The problem in education is that the results of gender bias influence the decisions students make in the courses they take, which in turn influences, and ultimately may limit, their career choices. In reality, this influence is a serious career determining issue and the more that educators work to eliminate bias the more career opportunities we open to students, regardless of their gender.

It appears that the seeds of gender bias appear in the shaping of one's mind, similar to programming a computer, from birth and on. We tend to learn what we live and we live what we learn. Unfortunately, some positive intentions done as parents, teachers, role models, etc. have unknowing, unrealistic, and sometimes negative consequences. This Chapter will specifically focus on gender biases from home and in education, and their effects.

Gender Bias at Home

Education statistics indicate there are fewer females in math and science related disciplines because of differences either in social practices between men and women, personal/family obligations, the way math and science are taught in elementary and secondary education, and traditional advisement in schools. Collectively all of these situations appear to contribute to the under-representation of females in science related education versus their male counterparts.

The social issues begin early in family life with different role expectations between boys and girls. Examples of expectations begin with boys whose expectations are many times perceived and vocalized by their parents to grow up to be in more masculine perceived occupations such as builders, tradesmen, engineers, sports players, etc. Whereas girls are many times perceived and vocalized to grow up to be in more feminine perceived occupations such as models, nurses, secretaries, elementary school teachers, or less masculine fields. These roles, too many times, are self-fulfilling in that individuals try to become what is expected of them.

Unfortunately, what is expected of children is too many times perceived from tradition rather than logical ability. Girls and boys have similar scholastic abilities yet are steered by biases and tradition rather than generated interest. Additional factors relating to the way gender is differentiated are often times related to geographical norms, religious beliefs, family economics, ethnic and racial backgrounds, etc. It appears that all of these factors tend to promote unbalanced career choices resulting in many students not becoming what they are capable of being, or really interested in being.

Gender Bias at School

In school, gender biases tend to increase unnoticed but in themselves are a very strong influence in course and curriculum decision making. Subsequently this influences the student's life altering career decisions.

Gender bias begins in the elementary school and continues to the secondary level, and so on. For the most part the coursework developed at these levels is not developed to attract female curiosity. Most lessons presented in the classroom are unknowingly gender biased as historical contributions made by females in science are not emphasized in the curriculum, versus their male counterparts, nor is the course material presented to accommodate the different learning styles of females.

The first real educational barrier encountered by female students is the challenge of the math and science curriculums. Investigation shows little bias in the early elementary years, but in the middle school females begin to show a more negative attitude toward math and science than males. This is a glaring example of needing continuous improvement in the more difficult subjects which would then attract students rather than generate the fear that they do. If math and science courses were designed and taught to generate greater student interest, and presented multi-mode to enhance learning, they would attract more students.

In reality, females in general have fewer science related experiences than males do. Males have a substantially greater history of working with or fixing something electrical/mechanical than females do. Overall, females are not exposed to toys and activities that ignite their curiosity about science and tend to be less exposed to science in general. This disinterest in science, and resultant math requirements, leads females to avoid taking the advanced courses necessary for careers in science. When they graduate from high school they are not academically equipped or motivated to pursue careers in science or engineering. Therefore, fewer females enroll in science related programs after they finish high school. It is logical that to lessen/eliminate gender bias in middle and high school curriculums the teachers need to address the interests and learning styles of females. Additionally, the contributions made by women have to be acknowledged in order to maintain female interest. Herein, as most scientists are male, science traditionally has represented a male point of view. Teaching becomes less gender biased when focused more on concerns with social significance and less on specialized mechanical applications. Additionally, solving problems more traditionally female oriented and using less gender biased language allow females to feel less alienated by the process. Examples used in the classroom such as the trajectory of a spacecraft or the mechanical workings of a car are gender biased and few females can relate to the subject matter from prior experience. Because females cannot readily relate to the material they lose interest and gravitate towards subjects which they feel more relevance.

Advisement Bias

Conventional advisement in school has its own biases. Studies of junior high school students show that many male and female students are unaware of career options available to them as well as their educational requirements. Much school advisement and career advisement is predicated on past grades and coursework and this is then used as an inaccurate predictor of future options and success. Thus, many are counseled into traditional career tracks rather than areas of genuine interest; which would necessitate problem solving with the student on how and what to do to achieve interests and goals. As a former statistics professor once indicated: "national studies conducted to follow students from school to work in order to predict outcomes, based on hundreds of variables, could only confidently reveal that boys could lift heavier weights than girls. Any other variable relationships had minimal levels of significance and were sheer speculation."

> Student advisement based on past performance is time poorly spent. It is negative because it plants the seed "I can only become something based on what I have already done."

This type of thinking has to be abolished in education. Note that people tend to do well at what they want to do, and the converse seemingly holds true.

Example: A borderline performing college student always sat in the rear of the class, informally dressed, and appeared to be constantly physically exhausted. At the end of his last semester the Department Head, who was one of his final class teachers, had to decide his course grade which border-lined on a C to a D (A letter grade of D in the student's major field of study would prevent graduation requiring the student to repeat the course). Having documented course work that fell in the area of C grading, more

CHAPTER 6: ELIMINATION OF GENDER BIAS

so then D grading, the final grade of C was assigned.

After graduation some students stay on campus for employment interviews with prospective employers. The Department Head took a few vacation days during which time he received a call from the Department Secretary. The Secretary, who scheduled interviews for the employers, said that the department's largest employer (A large national Aero-Space company) wanted to interview any remaining graduates so she scheduled the "borderline" student *in opposition to customary minimum required GPA (grade point average) for interviews* and also one of the department's higher GPA graduates. The reason the Secretary called the Department Head was to alert him that they were the only two graduates remaining on campus at the time and she did not want to disappoint the company interviewers. The final outcome was that both were hired which made the Department Head a little tense as this company was very specific about the high-performance expectations of their employees—and low-level job performance would relate back to the academic department and institution.

About 10 months later a prior graduate who was employed by the Aero-Space company and had advanced to a higher management position within the company stopped in to say hello to the Department Head. He wanted to thank the Department Head for the graduates they hired, specifically one of the two, last year. He said that the higher GPA student was doing well but the other one was exceptional and was already promoted to training new employees on their proprietary computer program which was notoriously difficult to learn. The Department Head wondered—are we talking about the same person? Yes, it was the "borderline" student and his employers felt he was exceptional and they wanted to thank the Department Head for his academic preparation and interview. The prior graduate who was relating all this said they only had one issue with him and that was they could not get him to take off his necktie.

Most companies in the warmer climate of the southwest U.S. prefer their office employees to wear open collars unless meetings dictate otherwise. This employee apparently preferred to wear his necktie. Again, the former graduate thanked the Department Head and left.

About a year later the Department Secretary indicated the prior "borderline" graduate was visiting the area and wanted to say hello to the Department Head. The Department Head welcomed him into his office and asked him how he liked his job, to which he responded. "You know Dr. ...., all my life growing up in the southwest I never had a white shirt, or tie, or suit jacket. I always wanted a job where I could dress professionally and because of you I was able to do that so I wanted to thank you in person". It was also revealed that he worked two jobs when going to school and was physically exhausted (lack of sleep) when attending class. The Department Head was enlightened from the prior student's story that verified the notion that trying to predict a person's future or performance is wasted energy. The Department Head thanked the graduate for the visit and wished him the best of everything. There is a moral here and is purposefully left for the reader to determine.

ADVISEMENT AND GENDER BIAS

Unfortunately, some schools adhered to traditional advisement norms such as boys take "shop" and girls take "home economics." This is a typical example of illogical and gender biased advisement. This practice, occurring in the not-so-distant past, was practiced by very educated people. Gender bias exists in such simple forms we really do not realize it until we look back and recognize the ignorance of it all.

Example: A traditional advisement bias situation became reality when a female student had to get middle-school board approval to take a "shop" course instead of "home economics." The shop course consisted of one semester of mechanical drawing and the next semester of hands-on producing what was drawn. It was a personal interest decision that defied local advisement norms and required the permission of the school board and its president. The student was just an average young student who had an interest in mechanical arts instead of home economics. She, after significant persistence, received permission only after getting a male student to agree to take her place in the home economics class. Both students had interests differing from advisement norms. This scenario occurred in a middle-school and the female continued through the normal high-school curriculum and then went on to college where she received a B.S. Degree in Mechanical Engineering. Her acceptance of advisement from her college coursework faculty consisted of what courses to take to strengthen her math pre-requisites and was successfully contrary to her high-school adviser's advisement that said "Your math background is too insufficient in order to compete in calculus so try a less demanding career." It is apparent that the middle school shop course and her college faculty significantly influenced her career choice and resultant success; contrary to her high school's biased advisement.

Teacher's Gender Bias

Most teachers themselves are advising students all the time by their perceived actions, statements, looks, demeanor, etc. Teacher gender in itself is a perceived bias because there are significantly more men teaching in math and science at the college level and females feel in the minority for both support and true peer advisement. Conversely there are more females teaching in the elementary system with corresponding effects.

Classroom gender climate and a lack of role models all

seem to have a negative impact on female science-oriented students. At the college level, faculty are often required to conduct research and publish in addition to regular teaching duties, therefore females tend to choose a career in industry because it is more compatible with their family life. That is, companies in the world outside of education are more likely to allow women to work part-time. Subsequently, the absence of female faculty for peer support of female science-oriented students is a severe detriment to attracting females into science oriented curriculums. It is a well accepted fact in education that female students tend to seek advisement and peer support from female faculty and, because of that relationship, remain in and successfully complete an academic program that they probably would not have, had there been no female support.

As previously described, female students are less likely than men to choose a career in science due to a litany of reasons. Currently, females comprise approximately 20 percent of the science and engineering labor force in the U.S. but comprise approximately half of the labor force in total. The reasons for this disproportion are certainly diverse but gender bias from home, to and including school, are major factors. So, teachers, just being a teacher has a strong gender impact on the perception of students and carries a professional responsibility to promote knowledge and career opportunities emphasizing gender equality.

Chapter 8 Reference: Waldheim, M.L. "Comparison of Female and Male Educators," Research Proposal Review of Literature—EDD 596, University of Phoenix

IMPROVEMENTS

- Eliminate language in the classroom that promotes perceptions of occupations and successful people by relating to their specific gender.
- Reduce male gender biased examples used in problem explanations, solutions, and increase female related examples
- Increase, earlier in education, career that focuses on un-biased gender career options and\ the education requirements to achieve those options.
- Focus student advisement on what a student wants to do, and how they can do it, rather than what they are limited to because of their past performance.
- Increase female teachers in science and mathematics; serving as both faculty, student mentors, and under-represented role models.
- Promote female student organizations for traditionally male dominated curriculums.

Notes:

Notes:

Chapter 7: Ethics and Teacher's Responsibilities

A teacher must be both a Manager and a Leader and has the ethical responsibilities of both positions.

To the Reader: Apply the following improvements related to a Teacher's ethics that will improve student learning.

Ethics

ETHICS ARE PERCEIVED AS PRACTICING good conduct and having moral principles or values. More accurately the dictionary defines it as the "rules or standards governing the conduct of members of a profession." This definitely relates to the teaching profession and thus directly affects student learning. The effect that a teacher's ethics has on the perceptions learned by students is prolific. One only has to read and study the written student evaluations of faculty to realize the profound affect the values of the teacher has on the perception of the students. It is generally discussed by students that there are few classes taken where the teacher's political views and other personal values have not been forthcoming. Some to the outright extent that it could clearly affect one's relationship with the teacher and subsequently one's perception of the grade received.

Faculty projection of personal, political, and/or religious views is a breeding ground for deceptive learning and should be eliminated from the learning environment.

TEACHER RESPONSIBILITIES

It is well accepted in the education profession that the teacher is both the Manager and the Leader in the classroom and should conduct themselves at the highest level of perceived values. Remember students are learning from the teacher's perceived actions as well as their words. Personal views and actions relating to religion, politics, morality, and other controversially potential subjects should be avoided unless they are an integral part of the course being taught.

Where controversial subjects are a required part of the course, and discussed, it is the teacher's responsibility to present both sides of the issue with the intent of providing enough non-biased information so students can make their own judgments and decisions in a non-biased atmosphere.

In practice it appears that "ethics" seems to be a subject in teaching practice and evaluation that is generally avoided until a problem occurs and then critics refer to the obvious "ethical professional responsibility" of the person or whatever in question; after the occurrence. Relative to this there was strong discussion within at least one regional accreditation commission that ethics should be a required course in all college professional programs but that gained little support because it would require lengthening the program of study which is not a popular topic. The substitute to an actual new course was the accepted notion that ethics is a subject already "embedded in the curriculum." This meant that teachers discuss ethics as the need arises within the various courses of the curriculum. However, experience indicates that this does not appear to be effective, in light of the published number of professional teacher violations relating to unethical conduct. One only has to read the continual media reports of public teachers being involved in conduct contrary to their professional responsibilities. This type of non-ethical behavior has no place in education because it is the teacher's professional responsibility to *always* set a positive example of character and values.

The following description just about sums up ethics in education: A teacher must be both a Manager and a Leader. The manager of the classroom environment and the leader of the subject/group being taught. The ethical responsibilities of both positions are well defined by the paraphrase: "Managers must do things right—Leaders must do the right things."

Example: At the writing of this text there was a report of a U.S. public elementary school teacher having a discipline problem with a 7 year-old special needs student. The teacher's solution was to lock a female student in a room reported to be approximately 5 feet by 5 feet (closet of some type) with no windows and no interior door handle. The interior door handle must have been removed contrary to common sense, if not building code, because it dangerously promotes trapping someone inside without being able to get out. Reportedly the other students had nicknamed the room as "The Box." Apparently, this was punishment for contrary behavior problems. The student who was the subject of the report did not want to return to the school and so the mother visited the Principal who acknowledged that he knows of the punishment and "The Box" and per their discussion appeared to condone it by indicating "the room is used for special needs kids who are violent toward themselves or others." Also, the Principal cited lack of funding for special needs students, thus the necessity for "The Box." The School District would not comment claiming "privacy." The behavior ("avoiding exploitation, harassment, or discriminatory treatment of students") of those involved to condone such punishment appears contrary to ethical standards (AAUP); especially when given the common knowledge that physical punishment generally produces a retaliatory outcome.

The recipient of "the Box" does not want to return to school and the parent's concern is perceived as overlooked by the administration/school district. The School District, by not responding to the propriety of conduct, is suspiciously perceived by the public as supporting such treatment.

CHAPTER 7: ETHICS AND TEACHER'S RESPONSIBILITIES

"The Box" does not improve student learning—it destroys it by planting the threat that mental and physical punishment relates to one's public education. The student learns that going to school relates to punishment. This is contrary to improving student learning. Experience shows that the mental scars inflicted by such punishment will not be forgotten easily by the student, if ever.

Note that this situation is currently under investigation and only the initial facts/conditions, reported in the local news, were presented here.

> "Managers must do things right—Leaders must do the right things."

Chapter 7 Reference: AAUP (American Association of University Professors) Policy Documents and Reports, eleventh edition.

IMPROVEMENTS

▶ Ensure that faculty are aware they have a professional responsibility and are accountable to conduct themselves at the highest level of perceived values.

Notes:

Chapter 8: Evaluating Teachers

The foremost responsibility of a teacher is student learning therefore that should be the basis for evaluation and subsequent improvement.

To the Reader: Apply the following improvements related to teacher evaluation that will increase the student's level of learning.

The Traditional Process

IT IS LOGICAL TO EVALUATE a teacher on their foremost responsibility of student learning. Schools and colleges should be doing this to be the best they can be. The reality is that most learning institutions and school districts have their own faculty evaluation systems drafted and redrafted until approval is reached among faculty organizations, unions, administration, etc. The result is that they are very diverse in order to gain the approval of all constituent groups, therefore, a variety of categories make up the evaluation.

The contents of an evaluation can typically include: *First,* a peer evaluation whereby a peer faculty member observes classroom presentations and writes a report. *Second,* an administrative observation of classroom performance where an administrator observes classroom performance and reports, usually once/twice a semester, announced and/or unannounced according to the faculty agreement for that institution/district.

Third, a student evaluation of faculty which typically reflects the student's perception of the faculty member; and *Fourth,* a faculty member's self-report of activities, etc. All the evaluation items are generally put together and then reviewed between the faculty member and their supervisor and/or a committee made up of reviewers. The current process is very comprehensive; utilizing all parties concerned, consequently the most important focus of what the evaluation should be, student learning, is minimized.

Example: An administrator attended a required faculty review session where all parties gave their input and a reviewer in the group, who was appointed by a new rule asking for input from outside the normal faculty member's group, stood up during the end of the review and said (paraphrased) "after listening to this review this is a total joke." "This faculty member is not doing the job and should be replaced, but you people are afraid to do anything because you have to work with …… and you are scared of the union/legal/personal repercussions." He was upset and stalked out of the review disgusted. The faculty member being reviewed had real problems and should have been replaced but because of the review process (which subsequently supported and applauded his/her performance) continued in the classroom.

A faculty evaluation, specifically relating to the teacher's foremost job responsibility, should reveal the level of classroom student learning achieved; all documented by student evaluations based on comprehensive measurable objectives of the course. This is basic to implementing the practice of "continuous improvement."

In conventional practice it is rare to find overall classroom learning documented per specific objectives and then analyzed as part of a faculty member's performance evaluation, and subsequently used as a basis for improvement.

> The logical outcome of teaching is student learning and that should be the primary basis for evaluating faculty.

It appears this primary responsibility has been unwittingly diminished over time by layered administrative systems in which the need to follow complex procedures impedes logical and effective reasoning. Thus, school systems were able to shift the accountability for classroom outcomes to the consumer (the student). The system was successful at doing this because most parents, consumers, or whoever feel inadequate to disagree.

> The public's learned perception of a teacher appears to be not to question them or the principal, and to stay out of the principal's office.

Who, as a consumer, has the strength of mind to ask the teacher to show their effectiveness ranking documented by student grades? Students resist asking because they perceive the teacher may retaliate against them. Parents resist because they perceive the teacher may retaliate against their children. Asking the principal or instructional supervisor usually winds up in the standard answer, "We already have a comprehensive evaluation system."

PUBLIC DEMAND FOR ACCOUNTABILITY

As public demand for accountability increases the funding agencies (local, state, federal, etc.) will eventually communicate to teachers, administrators, and school boards and request to be shown the level of student learning and resultant level of teaching effectiveness taking place in the classrooms. It can be documented specifically by computing a class grade average based on a comprehensive final evaluation or cumulative evaluation grades; representing the student level of achievement of the course objectives. Paying consumers feel it is only logical that one should be able to see what is received for the money. Unfortunately, too many schools would be confused in that they would not know where to begin—no records of student evaluations tied to specific course objectives, thus teacher performance related to student learning non-existent, thus teacher effectiveness ratings not available. Due to our diversity someone in our nation's school districts is reviewing documented student learning and relating it to faculty evaluation and that example is the logical step toward improving student learning.

EVALUATION ACCOUNTABILITY

It is apparent that the lack of teachers being evaluated and improved, based on the level of learning of their students, is a major contributor to the learning dilemma in the United States. That is how schools and colleges unwittingly promote poor teaching and subsequent poorer learning. How many jobs/professions are there where the persons paid to perform a task are not evaluated on the outcome of that task? Very few. Even politicians are reviewed on the effects of their performance at the voting booth. Look at the professions of sales, entertainment, construction, transportation, etc. Persons performing tasks are evaluated on the outcome of those tasks. That is how whatever is produced is improved.

Example: The end of the Second World War brought

about a manufacturing revolution in Japan. After that war the products produced in Japan, and sold in the U.S., were commonly referred to as "very poorly made." People purposely looked for the signature quotation, "Made in USA," before they purchased, otherwise they were taking a chance on buying a product that would fall apart or fail. Then, thanks to an American statistician, Dr. W. Edwards Deming, Japanese manufacturing adopted an improvement process. In general, they documented what they produced, analyzed that documentation, and then made subsequent improvements. They repeated this process "continuously" and thus significantly improved the products they made. Their reformation from producing poorly performing products to producing some of the best products in the world is common knowledge and is an example of what can be accomplished through objective evaluation of productivity. Is this comparing apples to oranges; manufacturing to teaching? It is reinforcing the logical concept that to significantly improve what you produce, you must continuously document what you produce, analyze it, and then improve it.

What do teachers produce? The result of the teaching process is the learning by the student. That is the product of what teachers produce—student learning. Some protective organizations, faculty representatives, government studies, accreditation agencies, etc. can and do produce rhetoric that unwittingly expands the basic responsibility of the teacher;

so much so that the initial and foremost responsibility of the teacher, "student learning," is minimized. In reality, contrary to what protective groups relate about a teacher's responsibility, the bottom line to the consumer and/or parent is: "What learning took place?" In conventional practice the consumers pay the teacher to teach a class, the teacher teaches and no one knows what overall level of learning took place in the class. Yes, grades are given to individual students, but where are all the final grades, reflecting the achievement of all the course objectives, made available? They document the teaching effectiveness and resultant level of learning that took place in the class. Alternatively, the teacher has a record of all the final course grades given, however even that record (most often erroneous to verifiable student learning) is certainly not a primary and/or credible basis for teacher evaluation.

Evaluation based on verifiable student learning might take place, but it does not appear to be common place. First, to document what and how well the students have learned, and the effectiveness of the teacher, it is necessary to evaluate the student's knowledge and/or performance of course objectives. How can any process be improved, teaching included, unless what is produced is documented, analyzed, and then used as a basis for determining improvement. Again, the problem is that too many teachers are not evaluated on the learning of their students. Most evaluation systems of faculty are far removed from any documented learning that took place in their class. The most common related review is the "Student Evaluation of Faculty" survey that focuses on the student's perception of their teacher. This is far removed from documenting the level of learning that took place in the class. The learning that takes place in the class has to be the prime focus of the teacher and the level of learning should serve as the documented basis of performance. This information must then be used for improvement planning. To be a world leader in education it is necessary to continuously improve teaching. That is, improve teachers to promote the highest level of student learning given the objectives of their course; documented by formal and comprehensive evaluation.

Evaluate For Student Learning

Education has to focus on student learning. If educators focus on student learning, then the teaching that takes place in and to different groups (socioeconomic, urban, rural, etc.) will have to be varied and different to elicit the highest level of learning from those individual and varied groups of learners; different methods for different groups. The converse is obvious: If teachers continue to preach-teach, similar to all groups, then they will receive what they produce; higher levels of learning from those students/groups who adapt to preach-teach and varying failure from those that do not. The effect of this is a matter of a mediocre ranking and must be changed. One shoe size does not fit all and that must be the challenge of the teacher; to elicit the highest level of learning from different groups by utilizing different teaching methodologies for the different groups.

To improve student learning there should be an expectation that instructional supervisors require documentation and analysis of how course topic objectives relate to corresponding evaluation/test grades, in each teacher's course. The graphical representation of those grades versus objectives would present immediate recognition of teaching methods, where necessary, that need to be improved. That should be the major part of the teacher's continuous improvement plan. Also, the faculty member's class grade average based on a comprehensive final evaluation or cumulative evaluations, for all enrolled students, could/should be analyzed. This would document the student level of learning and the teaching effectiveness. The public perception is that they are paying for learning and currently cannot even find out how much, or how well, learning took place. It is not a convincing argument to the public/students that they should only know their own, or their own children's scores. The teacher's primary responsibility is for student learning and the teacher teaches a class, so what student learning (names omitted) took place in the class? **It must be known in order to evaluate and improve.** It also serves as a motivation tool to focus on student learning instead of verbal lecture teaching. It is time to reverse the roles and give the public/consumer the information to evaluate what they purchase. The bottom line is to change the system's philosophical focus from lecture-telling to documented student learning.

Public Perception

A responsible person is concerned because their child received a low grade in a course at school and approaches the teacher for an explanation. After a traditional conversation the parent walks away convinced the low grade is well deserved and probably feels guilty they are part of the cause.

On the other hand, it would be beneficial to both parties, if the teacher could show the parent the corresponding grades of all the other students (names omitted) and how those grades compare to their child's grades relative to each specific course objective measured. This would specifically document deficient areas and justify discussion regarding future improvement— problem solving instead of laying blame. Is this the only student in the class who received a low grade? If so, the parents could understand and accept that there is merit to the teacher's reasoning. Additionally, if the teacher documents his/her effectiveness rating for this class in comparison to the school's minimum acceptable level of student learning for a class (a class graded average based on a comprehensive final exam or cumulative test grades) it would lend credibility to the teacher's verification of the low grade in question. If the teacher would show the class examination grades (names omitted) then it would document if the low learning level of the student in question is isolated or a trend and thus verify the effectiveness of the methods of instruction. This, in turn would enlighten the parents, would lend itself to documented credibility and diminish alienating the education consumer.

The public's view is that they are an educational consumer in the world outside of education and therefore apply the common reasoning that it is best to "check the depth of the water before diving into the pool." If prior student learning documentation and resultant teacher effectiveness ratings do not exist, then education decision making to the public/consumer is just a gamble—and questionable. This will have to be developed in order to continuously and significantly improve teaching and learning, as well as meet consumer demands in and for the world outside of education.

IMPROVEMENTS

- ▶ Document measurable course objectives for all major course topics taught.
- ▶ Document comprehensive final evaluations and/or cumulative evaluations that include all major course measurable objectives, for all courses.

- Compute a "class grade average" using the comprehensive final evaluation grades or cumulative evaluation grades: all.
- Prepare a continuous teaching improvement plan by analyzing the range and dispersion of evaluation grades for individual topic objectives versus the methods of instruction.
- Re-appointment based on acceptable class grade averages in the most recent classes and a continuous teaching improvement plan.

Notes:

Notes:

Chapter 9: Teacher Contracts

To improve student learning teacher contracts should be written contingent on faculty demonstrating an acceptable level of teacher effectiveness (student learning) and continuous improvement.

To the Reader: Apply the following improvements to teacher contracts that would improve student learning.

Contract Types and Content

THE LEGAL CONTENTS OF TEACHER contracts will vary from state to state but the outcome of awarding a contract, and how that directly affects student learning, is what is most important. The public education institution and their teacher contracts should function specifically to ensure and improve student learning.

Typically, there are two types of full-time faculty teaching contracts used in public education—Probationary and Continuing (Tenure).

Probationary Contract

This contract is written for faculty who have not completed a probationary period, but are employed in a tenure granting position; better described as a "tenure track" appointment. Generally, probation periods for tenure track faculty vary from three to seven years, depending on the particular School, School District, College, and/or University.

Probationary faculty should be, and generally are, subject to administrative review of their performance prior to awarding every new annual probationary contract. The school's administration usually has the right to not renew a probationary contract without showing cause. In other words they do not have to give a reason for not renewing a contract and can terminate the faculty employment whenever and for whatever they choose. However, this is not always the case in a probationary contract as a faculty member in say the 5th or 6th year of a 7 year tenure granting position has gained legal support in some states for requiring the institution to show cause, even though they are not legally bound to do that. The reasoning for this is if the institution has employed them for four years or so without documented problems, meaning their performance was acceptable, they should be given the chance to correct any deficiencies cited before the tenure decision. Therefore, the early years in the probationary appointment are now being focused on more intently. Also, once the faculty member has completed the probationary process and is tenured (tenure decisions vary among institutions from somewhat automatic to exceedingly selective) it is the school's responsibility to show cause for non-contract renewal. This process can be, and generally is, a huge and significant impediment to student learning. A faculty member who completes the probationary period and is not awarded tenure usually ends their employment at that institution

Continuing Contract (Tenure)

This contract is an automatic contract awarded annually and continuously. It is important to acknowledge that many tenured faculty are very professional and excel in their academic responsibilities. The problems related to tenure tend to occur with a minor amount of tenured faculty, but take up an enormous amount of administrative time, legal proceedings, and create significant dissention and distraction—all contrary to student learning. Thus, the negative public perception and notoriety of the term "Tenure."

The legal process of non-acceptable tenured faculty performance is so involved and time delaying that most schools avoid it. In effect, the most often occurring way a tenured faculty member is terminated is when the faculty member commits a felony, then they are placed on administrative leave pending the outcome of the public judicial process. If convicted of a felony, they are terminated. If not convicted the tenured faculty member generally resumes their school duties. Any non-acceptable performance, other than the commission of a felony, is disputable and winds up in lengthy review between the tenured faculty member and the school administration. More often than not this process takes years to work through given that the school must provide remedial education and/or training for the tenured faculty member based on the accepted concept that the faculty member's performance during the probationary period was acceptable, and because it is not acceptable now, must be the responsibility of the school. Thus, the school must provide remedial education and/or training to bring the poor performance back from deficient to acceptable.

Ineffective performance of tenured teachers tends to include poor classroom teaching documented by low levels of student learning, resistance to course and program revisions including incorporating new technology and other curriculum changes advised by external advisory groups and/or school administration. Such resistance to changes results in promoting student learning obsolescence and initiates the start of a lengthy legal show cause complaint against the faculty member. This legal process usually winds up causing polarization of faculty supporters/non-supporters which increases internally due to the lengthy duration of the legal proceedings. Many times the end result appears to be worse than the initial problem itself and that is one of the major reasons that school administrations do not pursue specific and necessary staffing changes. Legal avoidance of deficient performance promotes and leads to obsolescence, the opposite of the concept of continuous improvement. It is a reality that teacher tenure is a current contractual situation that hinders school administration from acting to resolve deficient performance and thus is an unintended impediment to student learning.

There is also the influential effect of a continuous employment contract (tenure):

Example: Katherine, a 5th grade student at the local public elementary school came home in tears saying she was moved to a remedial reading group in her class and she didn't think that she should be there—"It was boring." Her mother was concerned because both of her daughters were prolific readers, imitating their father who was studying every evening for an advanced degree. The next day the mother, a non-confrontational person, met with the class teacher after school and expressed her daughter's concern. The teacher was adamant about her decision to which the mother asked how she made the determination. The reply was short and descriptive: "my 20 years experience, that's how."

The conversation was ended and the mother retreated not knowing what the reading problems actually were. A few days later Katherine's father spoke to the principal about the issue and was confronted with the fact that the teacher was tenured and as such her determination for placement in remedial reading was in the best interest of the student and should not be questioned due to her experience.

That conversation led to Katherine's transfer to a small

church related private school in the area where she lived. About the second week of classes the Principal of the new school called Katherine's father and asked him to stop in after work. The Principal said that the State has a reading specialist that visits their private school every two weeks to test any new students for placement and also to work with any other problematic student reading issues. He said the issue with Katherine was that she tested off the charts in the placement test (which is designed for students not to do) and either it was a quirk of guessing, or whatever, so the reading specialist was returning next week to re-test her for placement. The next week the Principal called Katherine's father again and said that the specialist, after retesting for reading and comprehension, placed Katherine at the sophomore high school level. This whole situation was only generated by a person who would not be questioned because of continuing contract status (tenure).

The tenured teacher was never even informed or responded to the ensuing placement. This is an example of the assertive influence that tenured faculty have established in the system due to their continuous contract status. Had the faculty member not been tenured the justification for making the remedial reading decision would, more likely than not, have been justified by more objective means such as testing. There should be accountability tied to continuous contracts instead of unquestioned influence due to near permanent job status.

Faculty associations indicate that the foremost and justifiable arguments in favor of tenure are:
- Protection from being fired for personal, political, or similar reasons.
- Stops schools from replacing high-cost teachers with low cost new teachers.
- Protects teachers for teaching controversial topics.
- Promises a secure profession.
- Protects faulty by lay-off related to and by seniority.
- A reward for positive and continuous prior teaching evaluations.

> Currently there appears to be no relationship to documented student learning in the tenure arguments/reasons and that is the primary job responsibility of the teacher.

Thus, tenure benefits teacher's job longevity, has recognizable value, but is lacking accountability in its current design. Continuous teacher contracts (tenure) should be subject to documented performance of the teacher's job responsibility; producing an acceptable level of student learning and continuous improvement. This is a reasonable expectation and if the students are not learning at an acceptable level then require teaching improvement planning and implementation. Students move on, semester to semester, and build on the prior learning accomplished. If learning in a particular semester was significantly poor they are at an extreme disadvantage in the forth-coming class. Documented student learning, when below an acceptable level, and the subsequent negative effects, are rarely factors conditional in tenured faculty reappointment.

ACCOUNTABILITY FOR STUDENT LEARNING

The public's strong perception is that if the public is paying the cost of education (taxes and/or tuition, or both) then it makes sense that teacher contracts be conditional on the job responsibility of student learning. Proponents of tenure indicate that teachers are well evaluated by students, other faculty, and administration and all of these are taken into account in the appointment process. This type of evaluation process, in reality, is the nature of the problem. Student Evaluation of Faculty (SEF's) do not document student learning. They are the student's perception of the faculty member before the final grade is given. The relationship between a favorable student perception of the teacher and documented evaluation/learning of course objectives can, and possibly will be, quite different.

Faculty and administrative classroom evaluation of

other faculty has had subjective results and in reality is not an objective review of student learning.

Unfortunately, the current tenure process guarantees, for some faculty, the perpetuation of deficient teacher performance resulting in poor student learning and is one of the major causes of a failing education system. Many states do have a show cause requirement for non-reappointment of faculty however traditional union/faculty association bargained contracts just make the "show cause" process more difficult because the job responsibility of producing an acceptable level of student learning and continuous improvement is not an employment requirement.

The reality is that the more difficult it is to be accountable for student learning and continuous improvement, the poorer the education outcomes for students will be in that system (district, unit, school, or college).

Relating Contracts to Student Learning

By directly relating all teacher appointment contracts to student learning and continuous improvement the school would be re-appointing effective teachers, in that their students learn and document their learning through resultant evaluation. Opponents argue that the teacher's job is just not teaching. Teachers contend because their job may include meetings, paid retraining, coaching, counseling, study groups, professional organizations, etc., that faculty must have a spread-out evaluation focusing on all their duties. That is the reason student learning is seriously subjugated or overlooked as the paramount teaching job responsibility and is the nature of the problem.

The reality is that the evaluation winds up in a pro-rated evaluation that minimizes student learning to non-accountable weight of performance. Unfortunately, the whole concept of documenting what and how well the students have learned appears to be minimized. The actual documentation of what and how well the students learned is not available, ignored, or subjugated to a list of other so-called priority items agreed upon by a committee or bargaining unit. This job responsibility has been minimized through years by evolving evaluation practices that tend to emphasize everything but student learning.

To improve student learning make all teacher contracts subject to documented student learning and continuous improvement. The satisfactory amount or level of student learning will be verbalized, and will constitute major discussion. Subsequently the appointment of teachers will be based on what and how well the students learn from the teacher. There is no greater teacher priority or responsibility than of what and how the students learn in the classroom. This should be the only significant basis for re-appointment. If teachers were appointed on how well their students learned, the improvement in education would be dramatic. Student's final evaluation grades or cumulative evaluations, reflecting the level of learning of all course objectives and resulting teaching effectiveness, would be objective accountability.

IMPROVING TENURE

It appears that the major amount of tenured faculty at an institution of learning are teachers dedicated to their profession and make reasonable efforts to work with administration to resolve problems and stay current in their individual fields of study. The following are typical examples of tenured faculty members committed to student learning:

Example: A faculty member, Dr. Bill, was close to retirement and had been teaching the college writing course for a number of years and had written the text used in the course. He was an exemplary teacher who demanded the most from his students, and through years of improved teaching methods, was very successful.

At a faculty meeting he announced his retirement intentions and requested that his replacement be required to take his writing course—the course the replacement faculty member would have to teach. The faculty unanimously supported his request so the next semester the replacement faculty member attended all of the class sessions, took all the tests, was evaluated in the same manner as the students (with the exception of a final grade as the faculty member was not formally enrolled). The point here is that the retiring tenured faculty member felt so strongly about his successful teaching methods that it would be better for the new faculty member to continue on where the retiring faculty member left off, thus the new teacher had to experience first-hand the course teaching/learning methodologies.

This retiring, very effective teacher, wanted to ensure the continuation of a high level of student learning in his class—even after he left. That is dedication of a very respected tenured faculty member that the public rarely witnesses.

Example: A college Department Head had an unscheduled visit from one of the department's senior tenured faculty members. The faculty member described a student who was in his last semester, ready to graduate, and had run out of money for tuition. The tenured faculty member handed the Department Head a check for the total cost of the student's tuition and said he would like that paid under the condition that the student would never know where the money came from. The department Head went to the Admissions office and complied with the request. The student and the faculty member had no family or personal relationship and this act was genuinely promoted by the faculty member's perception of the student and the student's need. This story was never told or mentioned until now, after the faculty member's passing. This was a faculty member who earned his tenure status and never lost sight of his commitment to student learning. A real Hero.

Unfortunately, the problems that occur generally occur with a minority of faculty, which unfortunately take up to 90 percent of inconsequential managerial and legal time. During this time consuming process the collateral damage inflicted within the schools too many times becomes intolerable. People become alienated, faculty and staff take sides, others become involved in issues because of friendships and involve parents, students, and/or school board members, etc. Therefore, efforts to improve student learning by replacing or improving a faculty member who's performance is persistently deficient but is tenured is most generally avoided. The solution is to revise teacher contracts that currently have minimal evaluative connection to the job responsibility of student learning and replace with continuing contracts specifically contingent on tenured faculty demonstrating an acceptable level of teacher effectiveness (student learning) and continuous improvement. This documents accountability and by demonstrating acceptable levels of student learning with continuous improvement would help to remove the public stigma surrounding this contractual status and reinforce a perception of teacher excellence. Ultimately this type of contract would ensure improvement in student learning and promote a more positive public and consumer perception of education.

IMPROVEMENTS

- Identify all courses the teacher is assigned to teach.
- Require preparation of measurable objectives for all major topics in each assigned course.
- Require comprehensive final course evaluations or cumulative evaluations that include all major course measurable objectives, for all students enrolled in all courses assigned.
- Document a class grade average grading the level of learning of all major course measurable objectives and resultant teaching effectiveness for each assigned course.
- Compute the class grade average using comprehensive final evaluation grades or cumulative evaluation grades for all enrolled students.
- Demonstrate an acceptable level of teaching effectiveness based on the most recent class grade averages.

Notes:

Notes:

Chapter 10: Management of Teachers

School administration and/or instructional managers must promote the faculty responsibility of evaluating student learning to continuously improve teaching methodologies; thus improving student learning.

To the Reader: Apply the following improvements in the management of teachers that will improve student learning.

Administration and Management

What is "Administration and/or Management?" In practice someone should be the "person to go to," the person responsible, or the manager. In public education it is called Administration. Teachers report to an Administrator such as a Department Chair, Department Head, Vice Principle, etc. These positions are generally responsible for the day-to-day management of the faculty. This means being responsible for faculty/staff hiring, evaluation, scheduling, meetings, professional development, department events, budgeting, etc.

Evaluation

Faculty evaluation is the most important responsibility of the administrator/supervisor because it directly affects student learning. This process should evaluate teachers on the level of their student's learning and the subsequent preparation of improved teaching methodologies; all to improve student learning.

> A faculty evaluation, based specifically on the documented level of student learning versus corresponding topics, reveals the effectiveness of the teaching. The results of this must be analyzed, and improvements to the teaching methodologies planned, to improve future student learning--continuously. This is known as the process of analysis and continuous improvement—well proven in the world.

The foremost job responsibility of the teacher is student learning therefore a comprehensive student final evaluation experience or cumulative evaluation experiences should be used to compute a "class grade average" for each course the teacher teaches. This would clearly show the faculty member, administration, and all concerned others how well the entire class of students learned the objectives of the course and reveal the effectiveness of the teaching. The documented level of student learning must be the most important criteria in faculty evaluation along with the faculty member's plan for improved teaching methodologies. This should be used in administrative decision making and the reappointment process.

Traditionally there is erratic administrative response to poor student learning. The reason for this is that there is not a process in place to evaluate faculty on student learning and the subsequent improvement of teaching methodologies. This must be promoted in order to work with faculty to improve student learning.

It is public knowledge that our national high school dropout rate is disastrous; the community colleges are filled with students who had poor preparatory learning in high school accompanied by an additional number of prior student "stay-outs" who vowed never to return. Yet, conventional instruction continues in schools under the presumption that satisfactory (unimproved) student learning takes place. It is not uncommon to hear faculty remarking to others they have __ years of experience, implying they are a proven teacher. In reality, we have a teacher with one-year of experience (without documenting the levels of their student's learning for improvement of their teaching methodologies) and then repeated for the next __ years. This is the nature of the problem and is the breeding ground for an accelerated drop-out and stay-out education system. The faculty administrator should be responsible for requiring all faculty to have measurable course topics/objectives and a comprehensive final evaluation or cumulative evaluations to assess student learning of corresponding objectives. This should be reviewed by the administrator and the faculty member and be used to document the teaching effectiveness and determine the areas of need for instructional improvement—continuously improving student learning.

Final Student Evaluations

It is generally accepted that final student evaluations should occur at the end of a course of study and the elementary and high school systems (which are both a responsibility of the state) regularly promote various configurations of that requirement. It is also generally accepted this is not always the case at the post-secondary or college level. Many courses of study at the college level forgo a final evaluation, growing numbers to the extent that one regional accreditation commission now requires a "culminating experience" at the end of each course. Herein lies the problem: In order to document the effectiveness of the teaching we must determine the level of learning of the students. A most logical and ethical way is to have a comprehensive evaluation at the end of each course which is based on the measurable objectives of the course. How can a teacher improve if they do not know what they have accomplished, and/or how effective they are? It should be required of all public learning institutions that a comprehensive final evaluation or cumulative evaluations (based on all major course measurable objectives) occur for all students enrolled in a course.

These evaluation experiences do not have to be paper/pencil, computer, multiple choice, conventional exams, etc.—but rather evaluations designed by the teacher to utilize the learning modes of the students. This may involve individual or group performance tests, projects, documented investigation, or whatever the teacher can create to evaluate the level of learning of the specific course objectives. Students receive their learned information via Seeing, Feeling, and Hearing so it makes sense to evaluate their level of learning utilizing these modes as well. Logically the results would appear to be a more accurate representation of student learning than testing the traditional single mode of Hearing (descriptive reading and writing) although this may not always be practical and is not necessarily more accurate.

The implementation of objective faculty evaluation, based on student learning, is the very foundation of continuous improvement—for the teacher and the students.

Improvement in education, or any organization, does not just happen. It is generated through a process of analysis and continuous improvement until the organization (or whatever is produced) reaches the point its performance is publicly recognized to be better than anyone else and it becomes the leader by recognition. Without continuous improvement the contrary tends to occur.

Current Faculty Evaluation

In current practice, the most conventional faculty evaluation process used tends to minimally review the student grade picture derived from final evaluations or other cumulative student testing. The reason being that many courses do not have clearly written and measurable topic objectives. Those courses taught from a textbook can utilize the text chapter objectives, but a course final evaluation or cumulative evaluations should be developed to comprehensively measure the student achievement of those objectives, and to determine the effectiveness of the teaching. Where there are few written and measurable objectives it is next to impossible to clearly analyze student learning, and the level of learning of those objectives. Therefore, what might be reviewed are the final course grades from the final course grade sheets submitted by the teacher. This rarely indicates the level of student learning of specific course objectives unless the teacher has the evaluation methodology (the evaluations) tied to each course objective. There are instances where teachers might practice this process but, for the most part, the final grades generally reflect accumulated quizzes, documents, rewards, and the results of a generalized final test, if it is given at all.

The major problem is that teachers are not evaluated critically on the learning level of their students because, in too many cases, there are no measurable objectives tied to evaluative tests for the topics the teacher is teaching. This situation appears to be more prevalent at the college level. Even if there were credible evaluations for the subjects the teacher is teaching, the improvement and/or reappointment of the teacher by administration would not be determined on that data. This is because faculty evaluation is generally so skewed by other evaluative factors that student learning, if documented at all, would only be a small fractional part of the overall review. Where or when is a faculty member required to improve, or released, because of poor student learning? Unfortunately, the system unwittingly protects poor faculty performance and thus resists improvement attempts by administrators and/or instructional managers. Had faculty been contractually responsible for student learning and the conventional test or other evaluation results tied to measurable objectives revealed student learning was at a less than acceptable level, the administration would have documentation to support necessary improvement. In too many cases faculty have continuing appointment based on unwitting evaluation, are not contractually responsible for documenting student learning and subsequent improvement, and the school system (given the legal roadblocks) would not even attempt requiring documented improvement in teaching methods. Therefore, teaching depreciates, learning depreciates, students drop out, and the public questions why our schools have the problems that they have. In reaction, the government legislates more money into the system (programs, initiatives, etc.) and winds up with the same result. That is why legislating more money into an operationally deficient system will not work. The public educational system needs continuous improvement of instructional methodologies to remain current for learner's physical, technological, and societal changes—preparing for the changing world outside of education.

It is reality that operationally our current public educational system unintentionally protects poor teaching that results in poor student learning. This is just the opposite of what reasonable parents, taxpayers, educational leaders, or interested people want. To improve student learning teachers should be accountable for their job responsibility, specifically "student learning." Then, measure their effectiveness by documenting and analyzing the student learning that took place. Based on that analysis, make changes to improve future student learning (improve the methods of instruction) and continue the process as the major part of a faculty member's appointment. This, initially, might be a resisted practice because it is intimidating the status-quo. Fortunately, there are teachers who would welcome it, do not see it as intimidation because their teaching goal is student learning. If their students were not learning, the way they wanted them to, they would make immediate instructional improvements in order to have their students learn. Anything less would be an insult to their ability—*they are the few and the proud.* It is public knowledge that many parents, students, educators, lawmakers and other critics of education do not support the teaching and resultant learning practices in the conventional public system. They see the resultant deficiencies but are restricted by rules and negotiated contractual terms appearing too difficult to change.

Perception of Improvement

Begin with accepting the concept the most important person in the classroom is the student—what they learn, and at what level they learn. Most will acknowledge the student is the most important person, but the real issue will be "at what level they learn." This will be resisted with the perpetual argument: "teachers teach and it is up to the students as individuals to learn." This argument is false as it is a well proven reality that the way a teacher teaches determines student learning. This argument also leads to teacher complacency, apathy, and is the major problem we face, not the solution. The good teachers have the common goal of student learning as their main purpose in the classroom. Not because someone told them to, but because they believe it is their professional responsibility as a teacher. This seems to be the common value of those teachers who receive awards for excellent teaching. So then, at what level the students learn should be the primary concern of everyone. That primary concern must be the primary responsibility of the employed teacher. The teacher should be evaluated on their student's level of learning. To do this, many current accepted practices will have to be improved. Measurable objectives in all courses, evaluation of the objectives to document student learning, and teacher evaluation based on the level of student learning and methodology improvements.

Contrary to the advocates of the current system, there are few measurable topic objectives in all courses, we do not have comprehensive evaluation experiences of objectives (some yes but far from all), and certainly teacher evaluation is not based on a documented level of student learning and continuous improvement. The concept of documenting student learning and continuous improvement does not take away the freedom of the curriculum designers or specialty offerings of differing schools, it only holds the teachers, administration, and schools accountable for their responsibility of student learning.

Because the public is ultimately paying the teacher's salaries, and students make the effort to go to school, students and the public want to be confident they are going to learn. To the world outside of education, this is reasonable and makes sense. Everything contrary to this is just verbiage and has put the burden of the production of the product on the consumer, the student, instead of the product producer, the school and teacher. It is difficult to justify why common-sense logic in education evolved years ago from *"pay for what you receive"* to now *"pay in spite of what you receive"* is allowed to persist in our business/competitive oriented society. This perception has to reverse itself in order for the United States to become a real-world leader in education. The public has to be convinced and satisfied that it is getting value for their money. The operational process of analysis and continuous improvement is proven world-wide to accomplish just that.

ACCEPTABLE LEVEL OF LEARNING

A most important question schools should answer about student learning is: What is the minimum acceptable level of student learning as determined by a comprehensive final evaluation or cumulative evaluations "class grade average" for classes taught at the institution? How is it determined, documented, made public, and then used in the faculty appointment process.

How often or when has the public ever seen the total spread of final grades for an entire class? Forget about student names, just the final grades or cumulative evaluation grades for all students in the class and, collectively, how that depicts the overall level of learning taking place in the class? Never published, never talked about, never whatever. It is apparent that the time is arriving where public leaders will request/demand schools to publish their teacher's effectiveness for individual classes so the taxpayers and potential students see what they will be getting for their money. Yes, the taxpayers and students are actually paying the salaries of the public school's faculty, staff, and administrators even though the dollars go through a convoluted evolution of fiscal dispersal. What difference would it make to hand the actual remuneration money to the faculty, staff, and administrators (all in person) after the course was completed? The institutions would certainly respond more positively to personal financial confrontation and become less defensive and more amenably motivated. Because this will probably not occur in our complex system, we must have a built-in mandate of "continuous improvement" to counter complacency and its various viruses. This would enable education to function for the world outside education where strong performance and value predicts success.

The question related to student learning should never be: I wonder why my students are not learning what I want them to? The question should always be: How can I improve my teaching methods so my student's learning improves? *The answer to that is to apply the basics of how a person learns: Seeing, Feeling, and Hearing—in that order; improvements made continuously.*

School administration and/or instructional managers should promote the faculty responsibility of evaluating student learning to continuously improve teaching methodologies; thus improving student learning.

Improvements

- Document and make publicly available all faculty class grade averages and resultant levels of teaching effectiveness (derived by a final evaluation or cumulative evaluations) for the most recent classes taught.
- Determine the learning institution's minimally acceptable class grade average goal for student learning and teaching effectiveness.
- Ensure faculty have clearly written measurable objectives for all major course topics and a comprehensive student final evaluation or cumulative evaluations to assess student learning of those objectives.
- Ensure faculty re-appointment contracts are contingent on attaining an acceptable level of teaching effectiveness (class grade average) and a continuous improvement teaching plan.

Notes:

Chapter 11: Teacher Education

Continuous improvement in teaching, thus improvement in student learning, should be the primary product of teacher education programs in the United States.

To Readers and Administrators: Apply the following improvements in teacher education that will improve the student's levels of learning.

Education Programs and Structure

IN PRACTICE, MOST TEACHERS IN the elementary and secondary (high school) systems are minimally required to have a Bachelors degree and a teaching certificate, usually issued by the teacher's individual state. The teaching certification process generally requires the completion of a specific number and type of teacher education, general education, and major area of study courses. Faculty and professors at the community college, 4-year college, and university systems have individual higher degree requirements but, for the most part, do not require teacher education courses, including "how to teach."

Traditionally the faculty/professors at the community college level have Masters degrees and significant job experience in the subjects they are teaching versus the faculty/professors at the 4-year college/university levels who generally have Doctorate degrees in their field of expertise with less real-world experience.

For elementary and secondary school teachers, the college programs offered in teacher education are somewhat similar in nature but vary in structure. Some states require a student to complete a four-year Bachelor's degree in their area of expertise first (college major), and then complete a fifth-year teacher education certification program. Other states offer a 4-year teacher education Bachelor's degree program combined with a specific area of expertise. There are many other variations of education degree programs; the important point is not so much the variation of the programs, but what is taught and learned about teaching in the program. What is taught and learned in the program directly relates to student learning and this affects student learning in U.S. public schools.

Traditional Teacher Education Programs

Aside from all the psychology and behavioral related coursework the programs tend to focus on teacher presentation of material, generally through the conventional method of verbal lecture (hearing and descriptive reading). Education students do study many different teaching methodologies but tend to focus on verbal teaching because many of the traditional teacher education courses are taught using this method. Again, the programs do teach differing methodologies but conventionally practice the traditional verbal method of lecture.

In contrast, in the world outside of public education, teachers have been utilizing multi-receptive learning mode teaching for years. Within public education the traditional "general education" teachers (math, science, language, etc.) too often have not. Many of the "general education" teachers do not attempt the course pre-preparation and implementation work, incorporating all the receptive learning modes because they lack the real-world experience of how to apply what they are teaching. This is why so many teachers adopt the textbook method thereby teaching the experience of the author in a verbal format. This is great for verbal learning biased students but is much more difficult for others. Additionally, it becomes habit forming and the teacher builds their whole course around the experience of the author. Traditional teacher education programs promote and rely so strongly on the verbal textbook learning method that they overlook the changing learning needs of the student (physical, technological, and societal). An additional challenge is that similar teaching methodologies will not work for all environments including inner city, urban, rural, etc. Ultimately, the conventional verbal teaching method is a strong source of the failures, not the answer to the learning problems. Many faculty teaching in teacher education program are products of the lecture-teach environments and, in essence, are repeating what and how they learned. Common opinion appears to be that "if it was good enough for....so be it." That opinion is not popular with the multi-millions of annual drop-outs and additional stay-outs suffering the receptive difficulties of verbal lecture teaching—and who also will be the next generation of tax payers, parent tuition payers, and serious critics of public education.

Why are the proprietary private schools and proprietary courses so popular? Review the way they teach math, science, language, etc. Realistically applied, taught utilizing multi-receptive learning methods, by professionals who are experienced in the applications in everyday life. The conventional teaching method (verbal and descriptive reading) in many states is quite biased. This is why teacher education programs, and the graduates of these programs, remain on a traditional teaching format and stay there—regardless of need. It appears that technology changes rapidly, including student interest, attention spans, environment, etc., but human nature changes little, and in itself is highly resistant to change. This resistance is in opposition to improvement in teacher education programs and promotes a major part of the current learning dilemma.

Continuous improvement in teaching, thus improvement in student learning, should be the primary product of teacher education programs in the United States.

Effective Teacher Education Programs

Programs should focus on teaching teachers how to teach so all students learn. When do teachers know students have learned?

Students have learned when:
- They remember it.
- They remember how to do it.
- They do it.
- They repeat it.

The level at which they accomplish these steps will identify their level of learning (poor to excellent).

Overall and most important, the teacher's responsibility is "student learning" so teachers are responsible for all their students to:
- Remember it.
- Remember how to do it.
- Do it.
- Repeat it.

Teacher education programs should teach prospective teachers how to create and document measurable objectives (what is to be accomplished) for all major topics within a course or topic of study. Subsequent to that, and equally important, how to create and implement multi-receptive learning mode experiences (Seeing, Feeling, Hearing) for those measurable objectives—in all subjects and disciplines effecting all students to:

- Remember it.
- Remember how to do it.
- Do it.
- Repeat it.

Herein lies the most important operational task of the teacher: to do it. Teaching should be based on measurable objectives presented in an ethical multi-receptive learning mode format. This should be created and implemented relative to the type and situation of the students, the background and ingenuity of the teacher, the environment, and many other related factors. Those who continuously create and improve multi-learning mode experiences are destined to excel in their profession. This ability should also relate to textbooks. Textbook learning should be reinforced by the teacher's ingenuity to create multivariate learning mode experiences of the textbook author's intentions. Textbooks are an excellent guide, but the real responsibility for student learning lies with the teacher's interpretation and created learning experiences to accomplish the textbook intentions.

The real challenge of the teacher is not to try to change the students but to continuously improve teaching methods which in turn will improve the student's level of learning.

Interpreting Test Results

"Tests" to the student means "my grade." To the parents of the student it means "how well they are learning." Traditionally, to the teacher, it means an entry in their grade book and designates who the "good students" are and who the "poor students" are.

In reality, the tests really show the level at which the students learned the material the teacher was teaching and documents the effectiveness of the teaching methods used. The teacher must learn from the tests how effective their teaching methods were and then re-teach making the necessary methodology changes to increase and improve learning for all their students.

If student test scores are plotted on a graph, grades (horizontal) versus number of students with those grades (vertical), the conventionally accepted distribution for verbal lecture (preach-teaching) creates a Bell-shaped curve. This generally indicates the class has a small number of extreme scores at a high level "A" and a corresponding small number of low scores "F." The remaining scores cluster in the middle from B's to C's to D's. This is, in too many cases, the accepted dispersion of grading and is even used to unwittingly justify the teacher's proficiency. At times it is even applied to overall class test results regardless of percentage of actual scores attained—grading on a Curve.

In explanation: The test may consist of 100 questions

and instead of grading based on percentages (100 percent to 75 percent being acceptable grading, below 75 percent failing) the teachers use the highest number of correct answers in the 100 questions as a starting point. Say the students take the test and the best score out of the 100 questions is 60, then that is used as a "A" grade and quite possibly the corresponding "F" might reflect only 30 to 40 correct answers out of the 100, dependent on the other scores. Logically that means that the real student learning and response of the 100 questions was extremely low, but because of the grading method used, is acceptable and justified. Some cases border on the ridiculous; the best scores are so low the test should never have been given and the student learning of those topics was nil. However, in too many cases that is used and recorded for grading, implying satisfactory student learning. The justification for this type of grading is that the questions are so hard the students are not expected to complete the test so the teacher is finding out the point their students reached in learning the overall material. This is very deceptive. What the teacher should really learn from the grading is the level of learning of the class, thereby documenting his/her teaching effectiveness of the corresponding objectives and what instructional improvement has to be done to improve learning for *all* the students in the class. Because the teacher's responsibility is student learning, then the teacher's responsibility has to be to ensure the learning of those not learning.

Chapter 11: Teacher Education

> Tests really show how effective the teacher's methods are relative to student learning. The real challenge of the Teacher is not to try to change the students but to continuously improve the teaching methods which in turn will improve the student's level of learning.

Traditionally the overall learning of a class is camouflaged by only publishing individual grades to individual students. The real student learning effectiveness of the teacher is non-transparent and hidden in the class grade book.

Relationship of Necessity and Learning

Necessity and learning appear to be strongly related—well proven historically.

Why does the math class failure consistently understand and is able to apply complex odds at the racetrack? Why are computer science failures/dropouts interviewed and employed by major software manufacturer? Why does a science dropout make a major scientific breakthrough? Why are some of our most famous discoveries made by people not related to those specific fields? Why? Because in the world outside of public education necessity has consistently shown that it is the mother of invention (necessity promotes problem solving). Therefore teachers, convince students of the necessity to learn what you are teaching (through continuously improved teaching methods) and they will ensure their learning, not in spite of you, but because of you.

Re-emphasizing: Because the teacher's responsibility is student learning, then the teacher's responsibility has to be to ensure the learning of those not learning.

The real challenge of the Teacher is not to try to change the students but to continuously improve the teaching methods which in turn will improve the student's level of learning.

IMPROVEMENTS

- Learn to create and document measurable objectives for all major topics within an academic course.
- Learn to evaluate student learning (entirely eliminating curve grading) specifically related to course measurable objectives.
- Create learning experiences, for all disciplines, ethically utilizing all three modes of learning receptivity that affects students to: Remember it, Remember how to do it, Do it, and Repeat it.

- Learn to plan and implement teaching improvement by analyzing the range and dispersion of evaluation grades for individual topic objectives versus the methods of instruction.

Notes:

Chapter 12: Procedures to Improve Student Learning

To: Parents, Students, Educators, Lawmakers, and the General Public: What type of school would you choose? One that tells you what and how you are going to learn and the effectiveness of the teaching—all before you pay? Or, the current contrary? Choice can be a reality when schools adopt and implement the following "Procedures to Improve Student Learning."

Chapter 1: Realities of Traditional Learning

- Teach by ethically utilizing all three modes of learning receptivity for all course objectives.
- Measure, grade, and analyze student learning thus documenting teaching effectiveness.
- Teachers and administrators accept responsibility and accountability for analyzing student learning for planning continuous improvement of instruction.

Chapter 2: Methods for Learning

- Create genuine student interest in all course objectives and abolish threats of any kind.
- Ethically incorporate all three receptive learning modes for teaching all course measurable objectives.
- Create intermittent course evaluations to measure student learning and evaluate teaching effectiveness of all major course objectives. Utilize the results for the improvement of instruction methodologies—continuously.
- Display a recognizable classroom attitude and demeanor that the teacher's primary priority is student learning.

Chapter 3: Responsibility and Accountability for Learning

- Create measurable objectives for all major course topics.
- Inspire student motivation and generate a cause to learn for all course topics.
- Teach by ethically utilizing all three modes of learning receptivity for all course objectives.
- Document a "class grade average," grading the level of learning of all course measurable

objectives and resultant teaching effectiveness, for each assigned course.
- Compute the "class grade average," using comprehensive student final evaluation grades or cumulative evaluation grades; all enrolled students—no exemptions.
- Prepare a continuous teaching improvement plan by analyzing test grades for individual topic objectives and developing improved methods of instruction per the analysis.

CHAPTER 4: PREPARATION FOR STUDENT LEARNING

- Divide all major course information into measurable Topic Objectives.
- Create a one-page Learning Plan for each Topic Objective stating: the Topic Objective, Methodologies for Learning, Analysis of Learning, and Improved Methodologies.
- Create ethical multi-mode Methodologies for Learning for each Topic Objective.
- Analyze learning (the range and dispersion of test grades) for all Topic Objectives.
- Continuously amend/improve the Learning Plan's "Improved Methodologies" based on the Analysis of Learning—each time a Topic Objective is taught.

Chapter 5: Evaluation of Student Learning

- Create student evaluations of course objectives when utilizing all three modes of learning.
- Grade all evaluations on a percentage grading scale to identify the level of learning of the course objectives.
- Improve the Methods of Instruction based on the level of learning of course objectives identified in the evaluations.
- Evaluate and improve the Methods of Instruction continuously.

Chapter 6: Elimination of Gender Bias

- Eliminate language in the classroom that promotes biased perceptions of occupations and successful people by relating to their specific gender.
- Reduce male gender biased examples used in problem explanations, solutions, and increase female related examples.
- Increase, earlier in education, career advisement that focuses on un-biased gender career options and the education requirements to achieve those options.
- Focus student advisement on what a student

- wants to do, and how they can do it, rather than what they are limited to because of their past performance.
- Increase female teachers in science and mathematics; serving as both faculty, student mentors, and under-represented role models.
- Promote female student organizations for traditionally male dominated curriculums.

Chapter 7: Ethics and Teacher's Responsibilities

- Ensure that faculty are aware they have a professional responsibility and are accountable to conduct themselves at the highest level of perceived values.

Chapter 8: Evaluation of Teachers

- Document measurable course objectives for all major course topics taught.
- Document comprehensive student final evaluation grades or cumulative evaluation grades for all major course measurable objectives, for all courses taught.
- Compute a "class grade average" using the comprehensive student final evaluation grades

or cumulative evaluation grades for all enrolled students, no exemptions.
- Prepare a continuous teaching improvement plan by analyzing test grades for individual topic objectives and developing improved methods of instruction per the analysis.
- Re-appointment based on acceptable class grade averages in the most recent classes and a continuous teaching improvement plan.

Chapter 9: Teacher Contracts

- Identify all courses the teacher is assigned to teach.
- Require preparation of measurable objectives for all major topics in each assigned course.
- Require a comprehensive student final evaluation or cumulative evaluations for all major course measurable objectives, for all students enrolled in all courses assigned.
- Document a class grade average grading the level of learning of all major course measurable objectives and resultant teaching effectiveness for each assigned course.
- Compute the class grade average using comprehensive student final evaluation grades or cumulative evaluation grades for all enrolled students.

Chapter 12: Procedures to Improve Student Learning

- Require the preparation of a continuous teaching improvement plan analyzing test grades for individual topic objectives and developing improved methods of instruction per the analysis.
- Demonstrate an acceptable level of teaching effectiveness based on the most recent class grade averages.

Chapter 10: Management of Teachers

- Document and make publicly available all faculty class grade averages and resultant levels of teaching effectiveness (derived by final evaluations or cumulative evaluations) for the most recent classes taught.
- Determine the learning institution's minimally acceptable "class grade average" goal for student learning and teaching effectiveness.
- Ensure faculty have clearly written measurable objectives for all major course topics and a comprehensive student final evaluation or cumulative evaluations to assess student learning of those objectives.
- Ensure the preparation of a continuous teaching improvement plan analyzing test grades for individual topic objectives and developing improved methods of instruction

per the analysis.
- Ensure faculty re-appointment contracts are contingent on attaining an acceptable level of teaching effectiveness (class grade average) and a continuous improvement teaching plan.

Chapter 11: Teacher Education

- Learn to create and document measurable objectives for all major topics within an academic course.
- Learn to evaluate student learning (entirely eliminating curve grading) specifically related to course measurable objectives.
- Create learning experiences, for all disciplines, ethically utilizing all three modes of learning receptivity that affects students to: Remember it, Remember how to do it, Do it, and Repeat it.
- Learn to plan and implement teaching improvement by analyzing the range and dispersion of test grades for individual topic objectives and develop improved methods of instruction per the analysis.

Chapter 12: Procedures to Improve Student Learning

- Accept and implement this Chapter's Procedures to Improve Student Learning.

Chapter 13: Improving Student Learning

- Accept the reality that significant problems exist with student learning in U.S. public schools and colleges.
- Teach to the way all students learn.
- Apply the world-proven practices of analysis of learning and continuous improvement of teaching methods—to improve student learning.

Notes:

Chapter 13: Improving Public Education

The public's solution to improving public education has begun with some States allocating and/or proposing dollar amounts for each student's alternative "Choice" for learning—Charter School, Private School, Home Schooling, etc. The public's response to the absence of improvement in public education is to go elsewhere.

To the Reader: Promote and commit public schools to the practice of analysis and continuous improvement to significantly improve student learning, and thus public education.

Advantage of Improvement

THE BEGINNING OF THIS GUIDE began in the world outside of education because in the world outside of education experience demonstrates that holding the creator/producer of a product accountable for the performance of the product—ensures its performance. Imagine an auto producer who did not have to be accountable for the cars they produce. The public would probably be driving lower quality, high emissions vehicles that are more dangerous compared to the current vehicles; the responsibility for which is held accountable by purchasers, consumer groups, numerous related agencies, and courts of law.

What has become problematic is a publicly funded education system that is not accountable for improving the most important product it produces—student learning. In the world outside of education analysis and continuous improvement are derived from and applied to improve whatever is produced. In education *analysis* and *continuous improvement* have no consequence because they are not practiced (derived from and applied to improve student learning). It is conceivable that if education has survived this long without documenting and analyzing student learning, specifically for the sake of continuous improvement, think of what improvements could be accomplished with a commitment to those practices.

Necessity for Improvement

In most public organizations, a change, or more particularly an improvement, is "a hard pill to swallow." "It has been done this way for years and it has worked out O.K.—why change now?" Look around. Is what you see the same as in previous years? In current times concepts, products, media, environment, and the human response to change evolves so fast it is hard to keep abreast of even the language that accompanies the change. The reality is that because the world of education does not move with society's changing needs, those in public education will be progressively funded out of education. The invitation to seek alternative education and the availability of proprietary/ independent learning alternatives in the U.S., in just the last few years, has been phenomenal. It is too easy to feel protected when employed by a characteristically "slow to respond" institution like a City, County, or State. However, when the public seriously begins to question the producers of the educational product (student learning), because there are substantial problems with student learning, the public will look for and purchase alternate education elsewhere—and there goes the funding, budget, academic positions, and the school.

This process of defunding has already begun with some States in the U.S. allocating and/or proposing dollar amounts for each student's alternate "Choice" for learning—Charter School, Private School, Home Schooling, etc. The public's response to the realities created by the absence of improvement in student learning is to go elsewhere.

In Explanation: When the students leave their home school for an alternate "Choice" school, each take a part of the home school's funding with them. When the remaining home school funding is less than the cost of maintaining the home school—the school will be closed.

The Solution to Improve Student Learning

To resolve the student learning problem in U.S. public schools the education system has to confront two major realities: First, student learning in U.S. public schools needs to be significantly improved, and Second, the system of public education has to commit to a proven improvement process.

First: To be convinced that a problem exists in our public schools it is necessary to accept the realities cited earlier in this Guide including: mediocre world education ranking, excessive national and city drop-outs, adamant stay-outs, exploding school exodus movement, low test scores, and unpopular national initiatives. It is difficult to ignore that a student learning problem exists and for the future of our nation's public school system, needs to be resolved.

The result of one current reality of U.S. public education is that we are leaving part of the future of our nation to approximately four and a half million public school drop-outs per year (approx. 12,000 students drop out per day, 500/hour, 8/minute). Many in the general public see this more than just a problem—rather a disaster.

Be aware the COVID-19 virus eliminated approximately 365,000 people in the U.S. in 2020 yet we are limiting the potential academic, technological, social, and financial contributions to our nation of 4,500,000 former students every year with no proven solution in the planning stage except this Guide. This negatively affects all of us and is reason enough for even the strongest dissenters to agree this is a problem that needs to be resolved.

To any remaining dissenters the reality is that if the school is publicly funded and depreciating (loss of students and thus reimbursements), decision makers will decide it must be de-funded, buildings closed, and faculty positions gone.

Most teachers focus on their classroom and are unaware of what is happening around them. When faculty are handed their layoff notices the responses typically are: What happened? What was the problem? Why didn't we......? Faculty must be made aware and convinced of the student learning realities and the world-proven practice of continuous improvement to improve student learning.

Second: To commit to a proven process to resolve the learning problems in the U.S. it is necessary for educators to accept responsibility for student learning. *Education is a profession responsible for student learning.*

In the U.S. it is accepted that businesses are responsible for their product's performance (product's responsibilities), the military is responsible for their member's performance (member's responsibilities), public agencies are responsible for their employee's performance (employee's responsibilities), thus it appears reasonable to expect that public schools be responsible for their teacher's performance (teacher's responsibilities).

> **The teacher's foremost responsibility is student learning.**

Because the teacher's responsibility is student learning, then the teacher's responsibility must include ensuring the learning of those not learning.

The bottom line is that to improve student learning means to teach to the way *all* students learn, document the level of learning, and practice the world proven process of continuous improvement. These are the most important steps in *"How to Improve Student Learning."* Everything after that is merely academic.

The End

Notes:

Notes:

www.ingramcontent.com/pod-product-compliance
Lightning Source LLC
Chambersburg PA
CBHW060355080526
44583CB00012B/324